FALLING OVER RENO

The True Story of the Skyjacker's Wife

by
Mary Stevenson

Falling Over Reno: the True Story of the Skyjacker's Wife is
available for order through Ingram Press Catalogues
Mary Stevenson

Visit my websites:
www.marystevensonauthor.com
www.healingconnections.net
www.vedicstarcharts.com
and my Blog
www.watchyourstars.com

Printed in the United States of America
First printing: April 2015

Published by Sojourn Publishing, LLC

ISBN: 978-1-62747-118-3

For all those who truly love…
despite great odds

Introduction

R esist it as we may, we are all called to find our spiritual path, even if we are hiding under a rock at the time. Whatever rock I was hiding under when I was 22, I had no inkling that God's idea of yanking me out of there and into a new reality, would be with an airplane skyjacking! Every detail you are about to read is true. Sometimes life is just stranger than fiction.

This account covers a fourteen-year period of my life, starting on June 2, 1972, when my boyfriend Robb Heady skyjacked United Flight 239 from the Reno International Airport.

It is amazing that I saved all his letters to me from jail and prison in a notebook, these past forty-two years. Throughout my many moves from place to place, I hauled that notebook around in a box, never opening it until now. It was quite an experience to read them again after so much time. This process took me back to the emotions of those younger days. It has been simultaneously both a painful yet healing experience.

It also feels strange, and somehow perfect timing, that it is just now, so many years later, that I finally felt guided to write this book.

In these pages, I share how I was to realize that it took this tragedy to get me on my spiritual path. This is also our love story – a look at what we both went through to stay in touch and keep our love alive, all those years Robb was in prison. I remained silent on my version of events for all these decades. Now it is time to tell my story at long last.

This book is a recapitulation of my spiritual journey, as I emerged from the dark night of the soul caused by our sudden tearful separation. You know the saying: "*If you want to make*

God laugh, tell Him your plans for your life." It took a long time to see it all in perspective, but I had the help of some wonderful spiritual teachers along the way.

I hope that my sharing of this very personal story, will help others become more aware of how God is trying to reach them as well. We can run, but we cannot hide. Resistance is futile when it comes to listening to the voice of our own Higher Self. Don't I know, after having to learn the hard way.

What you are about to read reveals the deep spiritual breakthroughs that Robb's skyjacking and its aftermath brought about in my life, and how I was to become the skyjacker's wife.

Table of Contents

Chapter One
Two Plane Flights, Two Big Life Changes

W hy did he do it? I wanted to know. Everyone in my life was asking the same question. That included the two FBI agents who had suddenly appeared at the door of the friend's home where I was temporarily staying. My boyfriend, Robb Dolin Heady, was a nice, clean-cut young man from a good middle class family. He had no previous criminal record. He was just out of the Army and back home in Reno, Nevada, after serving his country in the Vietnam War. Those of you who were there and served in that conflict may understand his alienation and confusion better than anyone else. To most people, myself included, a non-political motivation for skyjacking an airplane is beyond their ability to fathom.

We were both only 22 years old and had our whole lives ahead of us. I had just graduated that same weekend with my Bachelor's degree in Anthropology from the University of Nevada-Reno, with honors. I had also been offered a University of Pittsburgh scholarship to their Ph. D. program in Anthropology, but I had already given that up in order to live with Robb. I was so looking forward to us starting our lives together, romantic that I am. The skyjacking cut our happy plans short. When I heard the news, I was in major disbelief. It was just hard to comprehend that he could do such a thing, and so shocking that it threw my whole world into a tailspin. Years later, I realized that this unfortunate "change in plans" actually occurred to push me onto my spiritual path and quest for enlightenment. Back then I felt that we were in love, but I would come to know what unconditional love really felt like. I also found the inner strength that I never knew I possessed in order to get through this ordeal. I didn't know then the term "dark night of the soul" but that was the testing ground into which I had just been thrust.

The date was June 2, 1972, and United Airlines Flight # 239 from Reno to San Francisco had been skyjacked. I was to learn that Robb did it. I had no idea that he was planning this. I was away at the time, on a weekend of celebrating my university graduation with some girlfriends who were all about to scatter for various destinations.

Nothing had ever hurt me so much in my short life, and I wasn't sure if I could recover from this. The sense of loss was so immense and the road into the future stretched out into the unknown with a seemingly endless string of question marks.

Would they give him the death penalty, which was a possible sentence, for this one senseless crime, when he had not physically harmed anyone? Would he get out of prison while we were both still young enough to recover the love we had for each other? It was rather clear to me that he was looking at doing some major time in the federal pen. Would his new associates in prison be a terrible influence on him and change him from the kind, sweet, and funny man that I knew?

I was also stunned to think he could put those innocent people on the plane under such stress, pointing a loaded gun at the United crew, and holding them hostage until his demands were met. That didn't seem like the Robb I knew. My heart went out to them, too. It still does.

How I wished that I would have asked him more questions about his time in Vietnam – could talking about those events have helped him to release some of those memories of intense battlefield events, so many of which I was not even aware? All I knew from him is that he had become a "weapons specialist" while in the Army. What more could I have done to save him from himself and this cockamamie idea of stealing an airplane and parachuting out of the Boeing 727 airliner, with his pockets loaded with cash, hastily gathered from the Reno casinos. How I wished I had recognized any signs Robb may have been showing of his confusion. I had no idea of how deeply his experiences in Vietnam had gotten him off track internally. Back then, none of us were aware of this phenomenon now called PTSD (post traumatic stress disorder).

Oh God, please help me. My mind was swirling with all these questions and emotions. I was shocked, confused, and upset, trying to digest the unimaginable. I'd always been a person of faith, but this trauma was to make me dig deeper and go further on my own solo spiritual journey than I ever would have imagined. While working on myself and trying to fight off the despair, the feelings of isolation and abandonment, and the growing depression I felt within, I would need to stay as positive as I could when writing to Robb, to keep up a strong front for him. I did not want him to see how devastated I was, because that could have been so detrimental to him with all that he was destined to go through, as a consequence of his actions.

I have much to share about what happened on the day of the skyjacking and in the days to follow, but I need to start a little further back in my story to show how I first got to Reno and met Robb, to give a full understanding of all that was later to come to pass.

It was June of 1966 and I was 16 years old. My parents were driving me from my rural South Carolina home to the Atlanta airport, with my two younger brothers in the car. Just to be rebellious, I'd brought along a copy of D. H. Lawrence's book *Lady Chatterley's Lover,* given to me by an older cousin. "*Oh yeah, they are going to be ticked off when they find this,*" was my thought at the time. I purposely left it in the car, so that they would see it. This was one of my "statements of independence" which I made to show that I was growing up, something my parents seemed to resist and just could not cope with.

This was to be my grand adventure, and I was scared as hell. My destination was Reno, to spend the summer with an aunt and uncle whom I had not seen in quite some time. You cannot imagine how shy and uneducated I was to many worldly things, having grown up in the rural South. When I got on the plane, I didn't look back. They put me in a window seat. There were two service men in military uniform asleep in the seats beside me, and I certainly didn't want to crawl over them to get out.

I was extremely bashful and uninformed about the facilities on an airplane. I wasn't even sure there was a bathroom on board! When the stewardess came around and offered me a coke, I turned it down. I was thirsty but didn't want to have to use a bathroom that I wasn't even sure was there. I was too timid to ask her.

By the time I got off the plane in San Francisco, from what had been a five hour nonstop flight, I was REALLY needing to go. The first thing I asked my aunt when I saw her was *"Where's the bathroom?"* She showed me, I made it in time and that was a great relief, I must say.

I wasn't sure what my aunt and uncle would look like, so it's a good thing they recognized me. We drove in my aunt's 1964 green Mustang back to Reno. They were such good, kind, and very educated people, which was to prove a wonderful boon to my own future education.

My uncle, Jennings Woods, was an English and Linguistics professor at the University of Nevada, Reno. My aunt, Marion Woods, had a couple of Masters Degrees and taught home economics at a local junior high school. She made lovely clothes and I was the beneficiary of some nice new outfits that summer. This was to be just a summer visit, but once they heard how badly I was being treated at home, they invited me to stay longer. They certainly knew my father. I got the impression that they always felt my mom (my aunt was her sister) could have done better for herself. Over time, I'd learn what dangerous pranks my dad would sometimes pull in his younger days, such as driving a car on the railroad tracks, with all of them in it. Sheesh.

I was ready for the change. It was quite easy for me to say goodbye to that first boyfriend back in South Carolina, whom I wasn't truly in love with anyway. Now I was going to enter a much bigger high school with a higher level of academic achievement expected from its students. I entered that Fall as a junior and immediately returned to the honor-roll level with my grades. They had taken a tumble when I was forced to take algebra and geometry my sophomore year in Winnsboro, South Carolina. I think it was only out of kindness that one teacher passed me at all. I was not used to making D's, in any case.

Back in the seventh grade when I was graduating from elementary school (we didn't have middle schools back then) I was chosen to play the angel in the Christmas play and that was a BIG deal. My teacher gave me a white satin nightgown of hers to wear, and all I had to do was stare straight ahead at the bright light in front of me with a beatific smile on my face. I was happy and honored to oblige.

Then the electric co-op that my mom happened to work for, had a tradition of giving out silver dollars to the two students in each of the two seventh grade classes who got the first and second highest scores in the IQ test we all had to take. The top winner got $10, and the second place student in each class got $5. I was amazed to be the second level winner in my class. Our top student, Martha Johnson, who excelled at everything from academic achievements to sports to beauty pageants, was the winner. My teacher later told my mother that my score and Martha's were just a fraction of a degree apart. So that made me feel good, but those were the highlights of my school years, prior to my move to Reno. My Aunt Marion and Uncle Jennings became my "second parents" and my gratitude to them is unending, to this day. I feel that they saved my life, on several levels.

Now there was a completely new culture to get used to at Reno High School, and it was one that wanted to make fun of my southern accent. Many times when I walked into my homeroom class, one obnoxious boy would mock me saying in a phony southern accent, *"Have ya'll had ya'll's grits today?"* I wanted to smack him one. The obviously misogynistic male teacher didn't even rebuke him, so I was left to fend for myself against the bullies. My solution was to work hard on my pronunciation to get rid of that accent. It took me about six months but I did it. No more talk of grits around me, please. The other students obviously associated such an accent with being ignorant, so it just had to go. Now that I'd pulled my grades back up, too, no one was going to be assuming anything ignorant about me. They were the stupid ones for even thinking such a thing.

I did see fellow student Robb Heady in the hallways at Reno High, as we were in the same grade in school, but I didn't meet him until later on, when I was in my first year of college. We started dating in April 1969. We were both 19 then.

Chapter Two
Meeting David

My first summer in Reno I met all of my cousin Jay's friends and that included David LaBarbara. He was a year-and-a-half older than me, and was to become quite an influence in my life, and the object of my unrequited love, over the next eight years. One thing David did for me though was to ultimately get me on my spiritual path, and for that, I shall always be grateful to him.

When I first moved to Reno at age 16, I was the proverbial "country cousin" and I had to get used to the new rhythms of life in Reno and its "big city ways." My aunt made my cousin Jay (their only child) take me to some parties with him and his friends, who were all three or four years older than I was. It was such a different scene than my quiet old rustic, rural southern life. I'd never had alcohol before, but everyone was drinking beer at these parties, so I did, too. That was not such a good idea for me. This was the late 60s, the era of sex, drugs, and rock and roll. I was certainly under those same influences for a while. I got briefly involved with a couple of my cousin's friends, over time. Then I met HIM.

Jay and his gang referred to him as "Lord Dave," this young man who apparently prided himself on being "a man of extremes." David had been away when I arrived in June. It was late summer when he appeared on the scene and stole my heart. He had stunning good looks. His heritage was Italian-American on his dad's side, and Swiss on his mom's side.

He was so intelligent, and had a high opinion of himself, too. We were all sitting back in the den of the house when the guys took a Book of Mormon and started lighting pages of it on fire. One of them had been raised in that religion so this was an act of defiance that they reveled in. Oh, big bad rebels that they were.

Another time we were at one of their buddy's homes when they pulled out some marijuana and started smoking a joint. I clearly remember telling *David, "My mind is too strong for this stuff",* but, er... no, it wasn't, as it turned out. Underneath David's smarter-than-thou, laughing response to my statement, I detected his admiration for my spunk and belief in the power of my mind. This was the beginning of my use of weed through the rest of high school and college. Amazing that I got the good grades that I did, smoking that stuff. It makes me wonder how much better I could have done in school, without it.

There was a lot going on then on the national political scene, and the Vietnam War was looming large on the horizon for many guys my age. That would later include David, and also Robb. What a travesty. It changed each of them so much, and not for the better, which can be seen in the "before and after" photos I have of them both.

My cousin enlisted in the Nevada Air National Guard, so thank heavens he was never called up to go over there and fight, and risk dying.

Chapter Three
A Weekend of Shocks and Revelations and My ESP in Action

R obb and I met and began dating in April 1969. After a few months, we broke up, which I felt sure was influenced by Robb's so-called best friend. Then after some time he called me and we got back together, about two weeks before he was to ship out to serve in the U. S. Army in Vietnam.

We had one very special evening before he left town. He took me out for a nice lobster dinner; we gambled some at the casinos and won a fair amount at the roulette table. Then he rented a motel room and brought in a bottle of champagne. It was quite a night. I guess he wanted to create some warm, happy memories to carry him through his time in the killing fields of Vietnam. That became the first time I had to watch him go away, not knowing if he'd ever make it back alive or not. I could not know at the time that later on, due to his skyjacking and long prison sentence he was to receive for that crime, it was not going to be my last time to have to worry about that. Of course, I wrote to him the whole time he was off fighting in the jungles.

When Robb got back from Vietnam, we immediately became a couple again, although I found out later he was also writing other girls while he was away. Oh well, I was the one he came home to. He got home in December 1971, when I was in my last year of college, and we began planning our future together.

At that time, I was sharing a two bedroom/one bathroom rented home in north Reno with a roommate. Robb had an 8-track tape deck with many of the best songs of the day recorded on it, and we'd spend the nights listening to those songs, and making love. We enjoyed seeing movies together, too, and then there were some camping trips that I was game enough to try, but those didn't go so well for me.

Here's what I was up to the weekend Robb acted on his misguided impulse, to make the national news with his actions and become infamous: I officially graduated from UNR on June 3, 1972. His crime took place the previous day, though I did not know about it right away.

I skipped my own graduation ceremony, to get away and have fun with some friends. There were six of us girlfriends who gathered for a long weekend at a private hunting lodge in Paradise Valley, Nevada, which is north of Winnemucca. Yeah, that's a big irony, isn't it?

There I was in "Paradise" while Robb was back in Reno creating a hell of a mess and ruining all of our plans. The Universe sure seems to have a wicked sense of humor, when it comes to me and my plans. That's something I've certainly observed on numerous occasions in the course of my life.

Well, this lodge was owned by the parents of one of my friends, whom I'll just call Lois Galliano. This was supposed to be a relaxing time, with two lodge employees who cooked for us and took care of things. There were no telephones, televisions, radios, or newspapers to be seen there, so we were isolated from hearing any breaking news. We were enjoying hiking, fishing, and horseback riding. Everyone was going to head off in different directions after that – some to Canada, some to San Francisco, and one to Europe.

That was a weekend of big revelations for me. Keep in mind my naïve southern background. Oh, I tried to act cool when four of them told me at dinner one night that they were gay and were in fact, couples. I shrugged it off, like, oh sure, I knew that, but no, I didn't. Later I was to learn that Lois herself had perhaps been doing some bisexual exploration, which came as a shock to me, too. That just wasn't my thing.

I guess everything in the next few weeks was to be a shock, one way, or another. There was that big "revelation" dinner at the lodge, as the four of them "came out" to me as to what their true lifestyles were. Okay, fine, it's just that I'd never been around any gay women before, that I knew of. I still felt the same way about them. They were my friends.

There had been a nagging sensation in me the whole time I was there, that I really needed to get back to Reno. I started talking about how I needed to get back home and find a job. I was definitely feeling some anxiety about that, the need to have an income. They laughed and said, *"Hey, you just graduated; give yourself some time off."* That sounded good logically speaking, yet something was tugging at me.

I felt compelled to get back to Reno, 205 miles away from Paradise Valley, which was a three hour drive. Something was internally telling me I'd better go home, and I didn't know why. At the lodge, I was sharing a room with Lois and we each had our own twin bed. Sometime in the wee hours of the next morning, maybe 4:00 or 5:00 a.m., when it was pitch dark outside, I woke up with a start. Suddenly I felt that something was wrong. I got up to look out the window but there was nothing to see in the darkness. I went back to bed, but felt troubled.

The next morning I kept repeating to the group how I strongly felt I had to get back to Reno. I had ridden out there with some of the other girls. Lois had a newer red Pontiac Firebird, a rather slick car. Finally, she just offered me her keys so I could drive back to her place where I had been staying for a few nights, saying she would catch a ride back with the others the next day.

Okay, then! With some pretty cool wheels, I was on my way. I had some country roads to go down to get back to the highway. There was a place where the road turned left in an acute angle, making an "L" shape. I could see the turn from a long way off but there was a big cloud sitting right on the road there. You may think I'm talking about fog, but the best description of what I saw was a cloud on the road ahead. Suddenly I was filled with fear, and I didn't understand why. I kept telling myself, *"It's okay, you're just going to drive through it. You will get to the other side*

11

of this." Looking back, I think that whole scene was eerily symbolic of what I was about to go through.

Oh, I got to the highway all right. In those days, Nevada had no speed limit on the highways, so I was tearing down the road in that fast little car, going 90 miles per hour. A popular Reno disc jockey, Pete Caruthers, was talking on the radio. He was joking around about how someone had jumped out of an airplane over Washoe Valley (between Reno and Carson City) with $200,000 strapped to his body. A skyjacking at our little Reno airport? Amazing.

Well, thank heavens he did not say the name of the suspected skyjacker, with me driving 90 miles per hour. The funny thing is, I was not putting two and two together, even then. The idea that that it could be Robb who did this, just was not in my conscious mind.

I knew Robb loved his skydiving hobby and was fascinated with the case of D. B. Cooper, who seemed to have "gotten away with" the first US skyjacking, in November 1971. My own feeling is that Mr. Cooper probably didn't get away with anything and never made it out of wherever he landed. They found some of the cash he took embedded in a riverbank of the Columbia River, downstream from Vancouver, Washington, years later. What a bad example he set for impressionable young minds.

Robb would later tell me that when he was in Vietnam, he had some dream of sitting in jail, playing his guitar. *"Well, note to Robb – how about not ever doing anything that could put you in jail, when you have a dream like that?"* But what did I know? I was only the girlfriend who had just graduated with honors after four years of study at UNR.

Anyway, driving like a maniac, I pulled into the driveway at Lois' rented house where I was staying. I didn't even bother taking my suitcase out of the car. I ran inside and straight to the telephone and called Robb's parents' house, where he was living. His sister Jan answered the phone and I asked for Robb. *"Don't you know?"* she asked. *"He's the one who skyjacked that airplane."* Holy shit, are you kidding me? I thought. My mind went numb. I had to catch my breath and asked her what she meant. The news was too stunning to digest for some time. All of a sudden, I felt like I had landed in an episode of the Twilight Zone.

Robb had stayed with me at Lois' place that last night before I'd gone to the Paradise Valley hunting lodge. I heard him let out a moan in his sleep and thought how odd that was. He had never done that before.

My dad served in the Army in WWII. Even when I was a young teen, he'd still wake up at times with a shout or a moan. In those days, they called it shell shock. None of our veterans from any war have gotten the proper psychological help they needed to readjust to civilian life, upon arriving back home. Post traumatic stress disorder was not to get that name until decades later.

Well, there I was alone, feeling stunned and in transition, staying at my friend's place, which she was also in the process of moving out of, so partially packed boxes were everywhere. Within a few short hours, the phone line there was tapped. There was no doubt of that, with the strange clicks I began hearing on the line. Things were sort of a blur for me, for a while after that.

I think it was the next day or perhaps even that same afternoon, when there was a knock at the door and two men identifying themselves as FBI agents came in. I knew nothing at the time about how these teams play a "good cop/bad cop" routine, but that's what they did with me.

Interestingly, I had no fear of these men because I knew that I was innocent. One of them sat there and stared at me silently with his steely blue eyes as though he were trying to burn a hole in me. They read me my rights *"...anything you say can be used against you in a court of law."* No problem, I waived those rights. The truth needs no defending. I cannot recall all the questions they asked, but I know the subject of weapons came up. Well, I hate guns and never want to be around any type of weapon. Apparently, Robb had become something of a weapons specialist over in 'Nam. He and I had been talking about going down South to see my family at one point. He joked about driving down there with a .44 Magnum like in the movie *Easy Rider* or something similar. You can imagine my reaction to that idea, even if he was joking around.

Mainly I can remember asking the "nice one," the FBI agent who was doing all the talking, if Robb could face the death penalty for this crime. The answer was yes – skyjacking carried that penalty in 1972. It was a federal offense. This was no small crime that Robb had embarked upon for his first and only foray into the world of criminal actions. I was so worried about him.

I told the agents how he had never done anything wrong like this before. I believe they were satisfied with my clarity and sincerity. They left, telling me not to leave town. I wasn't planning to go anywhere, that's for sure. Never before had I experienced such a desolate feeling. I had no one to talk to; there were literally no friends around. It was one of the loneliest times in my life. I think I just sat there for hours. Then the five girlfriends returned from Paradise Valley, and I told them what had happened. They couldn't believe it either. Robb had always been very personable, likable, and friendly, with good manners and a fun sense of humor.

Chapter Four
The Consequences of Being a Skyjacker's Girlfriend

There's nothing like a major crime to show you who your true friends are. Within the next few weeks, different people just disappeared out of my life, including my previous roommate. I think the FBI and police interviewed her. She told me she "didn't want to get involved," and that was the last I saw of her.

A few weeks later, I ran into Frances, one of the five friends from the Paradise Valley weekend. I saw her on the sidewalk in downtown Reno. We talked about Robb's court appearance, which was coming up soon. It was really going to be just a sentencing, since his court-appointed attorneys had him plead guilty. I had urged them to plead "innocent by reason of temporary insanity" but they didn't bother trying that. I guess you get what you pay for when it comes to lawyers, and these men were serving pro bono.

Frances just had to sing a few lines of the Tammy Wynette song "Stand by Your Man," in what I took to be a rather sarcastic manner. There wasn't much compassion that I felt from her. I didn't know much about lesbians then, but figured some of them must simply hate men. Either that or maybe she'd never been a real friend to me in the first place.

As time went on and news of this event was all over town, I felt further isolated. I remember talking with my Aunt Marion, whom I greatly admired, and to whom I was so grateful for taking me in when I came on that summer visit in June 1966. I lived with them from age 16 to age 20. She said to me rather sternly, *"Of course, you realize that your relationship with him is over."* Wow. I'll never forget that. It felt so cold, like a big slap in my face. No, I did not realize that. How can you turn love off, like some kind of water tap? What about love? But I didn't say anything at all. I just listened.

Why can't people understand the qualities of loyalty and devotion? It seems like these qualities are becoming an ever-rarer commodity in our fast-paced western culture. Part of my spiritual journey was to learn that devotion creates its own inner strength and invincibility. We hear the saying "Virtue is its own reward." I learned this through a lonely and difficult experience, and through pulling myself together with sheer grit, determination, and will power. This was a devastating turn of events but it surely did not mean that I was going to lose sight of my personal ethics and morals, my code of values for navigating this life. I remembered a quote from Shakespeare:

> *"Love is not love*
> *Which alters when it alteration finds,*
> *Or bends with the remover to remove.*
> *O no, it is an ever-fixed mark*
> *That looks on tempests and is never shaken;*
> *It is the star to every wand'ring bark,*
> *Whose worth's unknown, although his height be taken." (Sonnet 116)*
>
> — William Shakespeare,
> *Shakespeare's Sonnets*

I'm sure the whole situation embarrassed my relatives, and heaven knows what my parents back in South Carolina thought about it. My cousin Jay was not around and we hadn't had much interaction the whole time I lived at his parents' house in Reno. I'm sure that his only-child routine was disrupted when I got invited to live with them. My aunt and uncle gave me his bedroom, so he moved back to the finished garage, which had been redone as a big den. It wasn't until many years later that we developed more of a brother/sister relationship. I could have really used the support of an older brother right then. Oh well, that's how the karma cookie crumbles.

Chapter Five

Newspaper Reports of the Skyjacking and My Letter to the Judge

R eports of Robb's crime started appearing in newspapers. Many of these stories had a lot of inaccurate information. I'll explain the discrepancies later. Here's one example, from a newspaper called *The Age* dated June 4, 1972:

Parachute hijacker loses loot

Reno, – A hooded hijacker parachuted from a United Air Lines 727 jet over the Nevada Desert last night with a $200,000 ransom – but apparently lost the money on the way down.

Six hours later police arrested Robb Heady, 22, a Vietnam veteran employed in Reno as a car park attendant, when he walked up to a car which a posse had found parked in an isolated area of scrub.

A parachute, .357 caliber magnum revolver and clothing were found nearby – but not the money, which had been hastily collected from Reno's casinos to meet the hijacker's ransom demand.

Police said the hijacker apparently dropped the ransom as he parachuted in pitch dark from 14,000 feet – perhaps when he pulled his rip cord. They said it should be easy to find because the container could have landed only in a limited area.

At Heady's arraignment Federal officials said the ransom paid was between $125,000 and $200,000 – they were not sure of the exact amount.

Heady was charged on two counts of air piracy because two planes were involved. Both carry a possible death penalty.

Three other charges alleged interference with flight personnel. He was allowed bail of $100,000.

There were other articles, such as one by Brenden L. Koerner, who wrote the book *The Skies Belong to Us; Love and Terror in the Golden Age of Hijacking.* He had a feature he called *"Skyjacker of the Day: A Hundred Days, a hundred skyjackers from the sixties and seventies"* and Robb Heady was featured as #17. There was a forlorn-looking photo of Robb featured on his page, and the following description:

Date: *June 2, 1972*

Flight Info: *United Airlines Flight 239 from Reno to San Francisco.*

The Story: *A former Army paratrooper who was taking classes at Western Nevada Community College, the 22-year-old Heady barged onto the Boeing 727 as it prepared for takeoff. Armed with a .357 magnum revolver and carrying his own parachute, he demanded a $200,000 ransom. Since the local banks were closed for the day, United had to borrow the money from two casinos. Heady collected the ransom on the airport tarmac while holding two flight attendants at gunpoint beneath a blanket flung over their heads; this tactic frustrated an FBI sniper, who was unable to identify Heady and thus held his fire. Once he had the cash, Heady ordered the plane to take off, but engine trouble prevented its departure. Undaunted, Heady asked for and received a second Boeing 727 from United. As this jet soared over Washoe Lake, Heady jumped from the rear door, clutching a canvas bag containing $155,000. (He left $45,000 behind, perhaps because it made the bag too heavy.) He dropped the money on the way down and suffered wounds to his elbow and chest upon landing. He was then arrested when he returned to his car at 5:30 a.m. the next morning; the FBI had wisely staked out the car, which was parked near the lake, because it had a "Member of the U.S. Parachute Association" bumper sticker.*

The Upshot: <u>Sentenced</u> *to 30 years in prison.*

Some time later, Robb told me that he had landed with the money, and buried it in the desert, with a plan to go back and get it later. He just told that story of "dropping it" during the sky dive from the plane, to throw the police off. Under his lawyer's advice, he did show them where it was within a few days.

Emerson Marcus wrote one of the more accurate accounts in recent years, on November 22, 2011. In the article, he interviewed Steve Dundas, 70, of Reno, who was a United Airlines station agent at the Reno-Tahoe International Airport from 1963 to 1997. Mr. Dundas was working at the airport for all four of the hijackings at this airport, which occurred between November 1971 and August 1972. This interview offers more details than any other article, since he was a United Airlines employee who was on the scene that day.

Steve Dundas was in the backseat of an unmarked FBI vehicle driving 80 mph on Mill Street toward Reno International Airport with $200,000 in casino money.

It was 11 p.m. on June 2, 1972 and the hijacker was "nervous and making demands," said Dundas, a United Airlines station agent.

But this hijacker wasn't the notorious D.B. Cooper.

The casino money was for a man named Robb Heady of Reno. Heady hopped the three-foot fence at the airport, hijacked a United Airlines jetliner with a magnum pistol and, after the plane took off, parachuted out with the ransom money near Washoe Lake.

Three months later, Frank Sibley of Stateline rode a bicycle onto the Reno Airport tarmac and hijacked another plane with a high-powered rifle.

"Reno was famous for hijackings," said Bernie Crooks, who also worked at the airport for United Airlines in the early 1970s.

Less than eight months after D.B. Cooper's hijacked Boeing 727-100 landed in Reno on Thanksgiving eve 1971 — without him on board — two local men sought to duplicate the skyjacking.

The copycats

Hijackings were not unheard of before D.B. Cooper. Several occurred in 1968 alone — with several hijackers seeking political refuge in Cuba.

The model of choice was the Boeing 727 — introduced in 1964 — because its rear air stairway was easier to open and exit during flight.

"There was a little fin on the back of the airplane," said Crooks, who compared the 727's rear stairway to the exit in a C-130. "When it got into the air stream there was a latch over this fin that held the door up. You could engage the hydraulic system and push it right through that fin. The fin would break right off."

Cooper, Heady and Sibley all hijacked 727s.

Heady, 22 in 1972, a Vietnam War veteran, was a member of the parachutist club at Western Nevada Community College when he hijacked a 727 on June 2, 1972.

Dundas was loading the plane at 7:30 p.m. when Heady "came out of nowhere."

The standoff lasted four hours after a malfunction moved the hijacking into another United Airlines Boeing 727 parked 400 yards from the airport.

Two pilots and three stewards expressed concern that Heady was "pretty desperate" and upset with the "fiasco."

Heady, just as Cooper did, hijacked his plane after dark and asked for $200,000 in ransom.

But banks were closed.

Dundas, two FBI agents and a fellow United Airlines station agent headed to the casinos with checks to find the cash. They received $150,000 from Harrah's and $50,000 from Harold's Club, Dundas said.

"He wanted the ransom of cash by 11 p.m.," Dundas said. "This is happening at 9 p.m. We were scrambling to get the money."

Heady fired a round inside the plane and radioed police that he had shot someone in the thigh. He threatened to shoot more if he didn't get the money by 11 p.m.

"We were screaming downtown from Mill Street," Dundas said. "When we were headed back some man, an older guy, pulled out in front of us going about 10 miles per hour. We were going 80 or 90. We almost rear-ended him. He barely got out of the way. But we locked up the brakes to avoid rear-ending the guy and (the brakes) overheated."

With sirens blaring, the FBI vehicle continued toward the airport without brakes, nearly careening into a local restaurant as it turned on Terminal Way, Dundas said.

When they finally got to the airport — stopping the car with the emergency break — Heady demanded a woman transport the money. The only woman on duty was Helen Durant.

Durant, 32 in 1972, drove to the airplane and handed the money to a steward held at gunpoint. Heady foiled sharpshooters by coming off the plane under a blanket with two stewards.

"He was standing up in the stairs and in his hand I could see the gun," said Durant, who still lives in Reno. "He had a gun pointed at her. She said, 'Oh my God! Oh my God.' I just turned around and drove off and the whole time I was driving I was waiting for a bullet in my back."

After getting the ransom, Heady ordered the pilot to head south on a precise departure path.

"Heady knew what he was doing," Dundas said. "But the captain was sharp enough to alter the departure path by half a degree so when he bailed out of the airplane, instead of landing on East Lake, he landed on 395. It was slight enough to not make Heady figure it out."

Police searched near Heady's jump spot by Washoe Lake. Before he reached his vehicle, officials spotted a car with a

sticker that read "Member of the U.S. Parachute Association."
Heady was an experienced parachutist. The police were waiting
for him at 5:30 a.m. when he arrived at his car.

One of the above articles mentioned that bail had been set
at $100,000. Well, he never got out on bail, though he really
wanted to. His family had their concerns about putting up the
bail money. He wanted very much to see me alone one more
time before he got sent away for so many years in prison, but
that did not happen.

Portion of a letter Robb wrote me from Washoe County jail,
June 1972:

"....what I'm trying to say is that it would be such a great thing to
get out of here on bail, and really give my love to you, if you'll
have me and forgive me. My parents think that if I'm bailed out
I'll take off and they'll have to pay. I could never hurt anyone
that way. My grandmother thinks the same way, and people that
feel that I'm insane seem to be growing in numbers by the day. I
need you and love you. Love, Robb"

Perhaps I was the only one at that point in time who did not
think Robb was insane. I knew his thinking was mixed up due to
whatever he'd gone through during his time in the Army in
Vietnam. Prior to the August 25, 1972 sentencing, I wrote a
letter to Judge Bruce Thompson, who was presiding over the
legal procedures. My letter reflects my sincere naivety from
back in that youthful day, thinking that what I had to say might
make some difference.

"To the Honorable Judge Thompson:

Your Honor,
I have known Robb since April, 1969. At that time we dated
for four months, and then broke up. Just before he was to go to
Vietnam, in December 1970, we began dating again (for about

two weeks). Then I wrote him the whole year that he was over there. He came home in December 1971, and we renewed our relationship. By February 1972, we were closer than we had ever been, and I felt that I knew him very well. We love each other very much. I am the first person Robb has ever felt this way about, and for me, ours is the happiest relationship I've ever had.

We were much younger in 1969, of course, and our relationship then did not have the depth it has now. But at the same time, I feel quite certain that Robb would then not have even considered attempting the action to which he has now pleaded guilty.

Before going into the Army, Robb was a quiet, fun-loving sort of person who was not very concerned about his future. Then he got drafted, and was sent through the never-ending military gristmill which is calculated to turn nice American boys, instilled with humanist values from birth, into "patriots" hell-bent on destroying the "enemy," into murderers sanctioned by the State to commit the most gruesome of deeds, for which they would meet extreme punishment in civilian life.

I refuse to let this situation be dismissed with a wave of the hand and a sighed, "War is hell." The inhumanity of war and the military mentality is something we can no longer tolerate if humans are to continue to exist on this Earth. I shudder to think of the commonplace acceptance with which parents the world over greet this horrible warping of their sons' minds.

Robb was thrown into this sort of situation, totally unprepared of course, by his previous life and habits. He was taught to operate many varied weapons – for purposes of killing or maiming other human beings who were labeled "gooks" and implied to be less than human – the ever-present racial slur the military finds so useful in wartime.

He was then sent to fight in the front lines for months at a time, going without enough food and no sanitary facilities (showers, etc.) – conditions primitive enough to coarsen anyone. But on top of this was the constant fear for his own life and those of his buddies, the constant sight and stench of death around him, and that of the living death of poverty, induced on those whose homes, families, and livelihoods have been snatched away by others.

I was not able to fathom the degree to which these experiences scarred Robb's consciousness, because I've never seen anyone dead or even hurt in an accident. But I know that it must have made a heavy impression because he even took photographs of the dead bodies.

There is so much else I must tell you, Your Honor. Robb was almost killed and three or four of his friends were killed, due to the negligence and arrogance of a young captain.... To keep the men quiet, other officers informed them that this captain had been written up and would soon be demoted in rank. They later learned that this was a lie. Robb tried going through the existing system. He wrote a 30-page letter to his Senator (quite a feat for him) who sent it to U. S. Army headquarters. Robb was informed that there was no such report of this, or that experience (which he was present at himself) or learned that the report turned in was an incredible distortion of the truth. A friend of his who tried to fight such corruption was kept in Nam months longer than he was supposed to be, on one trumped up charge after another. This is of course, a second-hand explanation and much abbreviated, but I hope you see that Robb tried to fight injustice by the means established and was shown time and again that these means accomplished nothing.

You may be wondering how this ties in with his skyjacking an airplane. It is my belief, as the person who knows Robb best, that his experiences in Vietnam left him deeply frustrated, and confused about how one should live. For one thing, there is no doubt to any of us who know him, that this experience cheapened the value of human life in Robb's eyes: his own life as well as others'.

A professional might term this a case of extreme alienation or anomie. It seems so unfair to me that Robb is to be judged for a deed he would never have committed had not a greedy, *militaristic nation placed him in a situation which has had even worse effects on other young minds. I can't help but think of the case of Lt. Calley (*) who is guilty of far more atrocious actions, than Robb, who was under the same sort of tensions and fears for his own life and those of his friends.*

Though Calley was judged guilty, he is enjoying the sympathy of citizens across the nation and has special privileges granted by the President. Calley is guilty of murder. Robb stole an airplane. Which offense is more morally disgusting? Yet public opinion is currently overwhelmingly more interested in this new type of crime. The media fans every incident into a major news story. (I could write several additional pages on the effect this type of reporting had on Robb. I feel certain he would never have thought of such a thing if that first hijacking had never come about.)

Therefore, Your Honor, I have been deeply concerned over the sentence Robb will receive. I realize that the law insists on a minimum 20-year sentence. However, it is in your power to lighten the actual serving time and conditions of that sentence. I want to tell you that the one thing to bring any comfort to my mind this dismal summer, has been your well-known reputation as a fair man who is more interested in rehabilitation than in the retaliation punishment aspect of the law.

Robb is at a very impressionable stage in his life due to his age and his recent experiences. It is my strong feeling that what he needs is the guidance of those who love and want to help him. I have great fears about the evil influence of the hardened criminals which he would meet in prison. Robb is basically a very good and a logically thinking person. In fact, from discussions with FBI agents and his lawyers, from whom I learned the details of his actions, I can tell you that his mind was <u>not</u> functioning in its normal manner at the time of the skyjacking.

Author's Note: (*) I was referring to the My Lai massacre in Vietnam on March 16, 1969, when Lieutenant William Calley murdered 22 unarmed South Vietnamese Citizens.

If Robb were the criminal type he perhaps could have planned this event to the letter. He has the technical knowledge and intelligence to have accomplished it. Yet the very fact that he failed to use his normal logic must indicate his non-criminal nature. This was something he decided to do on the spur of the moment. I believe it to be a lapse into a sort of fantasy world he created in his mind to escape the gruesome reality of Vietnam.

There is much more I could say in this same view, but I hope this will give you the basic message I wish to convey. Please be merciful, our future is at stake.

Sincerely yours, Mary L. Stevenson"

Of course, there was never any response to my letter. I wonder if the judge ever even received it, since I entrusted it to Robb's lawyers to give to him. In reviewing what I wrote, I am struck both by my courage and by my lack of knowledge regarding how the political structure higher up in our country is able to bring pressure even on judges with liberal reputations. We later heard through the grapevine that such pressure had been brought to bear on Judge Thompson's sentencing.

The following report is from the St. Joseph News-Press August 26, 1972:

Reno, Nev. (AP) – Convicted hijacker Robb D. Heady was sentenced Friday to 30 years in prison for the attempted air piracy of a United Air Lines 727 jetliner.

Heady, a Vietnam veteran, had pleaded guilty to boarding a United Air Lines jet at Reno International Airport on June 3 and demanding $200,000 in cash and parachutes. He jumped from the plane about 10 miles south of Reno and was captured soon afterward. The money was recovered. Heady was armed with a hand gun during the hijacking and fired two shots. No one was injured.

Federal Court Judge Bruce Thompson said before sentencing Heady:

"This is an offense that has the country completely frustrated. Nobody knows what to do about it. The best method that is available to us is to use punishment as a deterrent. I consider it my responsibility to do what I can to try to deter future offenses of this sort."

Under the sentence, Heady will be eligible for parole after serving a third of his sentence. Thompson refused a defense request to recommend that parole be allowed sooner.

Thus began our years in the limbo of not knowing when he'd ever be released.

Chapter Six

Details of the Skyjacking:
He Was Lucky to Be Alive

I found out later that during the skyjacking, my uncle was listening in on some police scanner equipment he happened to have, as the whole thing was taking place. It was clear that the authorities were trying to trick Robb. They told him that the first plane he boarded where he was holding the crew hostage was low on fuel and had some mechanical problems. All of that was a lie, of course.

They were just trying to get him to walk out in the open, heading for the second plane they said they'd let him take instead, so that a sharp shooter could shoot and kill him. They were planning to shoot him in the head and put an end to this adventure. The one thing Robb did right in this whole fiasco, in terms of his own self-preservation, was that he put a blanket over his head and that of a stewardess and walked her with him to that second flight, his weapon in hand the whole way.

Was part of him still back on the battlefields of Vietnam, looking for some "enemy" to confront? Since I'm such a peace-loving person, I'll never understand that type of aggressive action-oriented behavior, I guess. I cannot even stand guns of any type.

He got on the second plane and proceeded with his plan. The 727s were the only model of aircraft that had an opening in the belly of the plane, at the back. I learned much later that Robb's plan was to keep all the staff up in the cockpit, a la D. B. Cooper's style, while that plane's bottom door was open for some time, and while they were headed on their course to San

Francisco, no one would see when and where he actually jumped.

Someone on board did see him, because at that moment the plane was making a slight turn. The pilot radioed the coordinates in to the authorities and the cops headed out to Washoe Valley to catch him and recover the money he had been given.

I really didn't care about the details of the crime. What I remember Robb telling me later varies some from certain accounts I have found online. Some say he had to leave on the plane $40,000 or $45,000 of the $200,000 that was collected per his demands. It's hard to imagine that he had not thought of a way of transporting it all down to earth, once he got what he asked for. As I said, he later described to me how he had not dropped the money, but told police that story to mislead them at first.

He jumped with just a reserve parachute on, which he had carried on board with him (he did not ask for parachutes, as that newspaper article said). I guess those are smaller to pack and wear than a regular parachute, throughout such a crime as this. He told me he hurt his back, landing in the wee hours along a road out by Washoe Lake. The press accounts say he hurt his elbow and stomach.

What he told me is that he buried the money in the desert, spent the night out there, with the plan of returning to his car parked nearby in the morning. This was the little white Triumph that I'd ridden in many times. Of course, it had a bumper sticker proclaiming, "Member US Parachute Team," which was like a glowing neon sign to the cops: *"Here's my car! Just wait here and catch me!"* Double duh.

He did not know at that point that any of the crew on the airplane had seen him jump and reported it, so that his capture was inevitable.

Perhaps when one is operating on the rush of passion and adrenaline, having lived for over a year in a non-real world of war, killing, and conflict, that's how one thinks. Lack of thinking, it seemed to me. Just plain crazy, by most people's reasoning. I knew that Robb himself was not crazy, nor a criminal, and not even a mean person. He was just screwed up from being in the war setting of Vietnam. There was no reorientation center for him or other veterans to check into when they got home, so they were plunged back into their civilian life and expected by all of us at home to "carry on as usual" as though they were the same people they were before going into war and seeing the horrors that they saw there. It's a patently unfair system, all the way around, in my opinion.

On top of all that, Robb should never have been sent to any tropical battle zone anyway, since he did not have a spleen thanks to a football accident in high school.

Back at his car, the police arrested him and took him off to Washoe County jail where he'd be spending the summer, with no time to go outside and get any fresh air.

I was trying to stay optimistic, considering that Robb was a recent military veteran with no prior criminal record. His attitude quickly became a bit more practical, once his feet were back on the Earth and he was confined to a jail cell, with a big prison sentence looming over his head. His letters reflected the feeling he was going to be "put away" for some time.

Chapter Seven
Robb's Letters from Jail Begin

W e were restricted to visiting him just one day per week
and that was through a glass window. His first few letters
from jail didn't make a lot of sense to me. First letter from Robb
from Washoe County jail, first week of June 1972:

*"Mary, Misery loves company and I miss you. If I would have
made it, you would have had your school and commune, and I,
my lake in Australia. I sure fucked up, and I hope you don't hate
me. I love you and need you, Mary. Love, Robb"*

"Huh?" I thought, *"What the heck is he talking about?"* I
would never want any stolen money to use for any of my
dreams. Where did he get the idea that I wanted to create some
school or commune? Perhaps those were ideas we'd kicked
around in idle conversations but that was certainly not where my
passion, heart, or purpose lay. Nope. His thinking was screwed
up from his time in the battlefield, not to mention all the drugs
he'd taken over there.

I remember he'd gotten very frustrated with some young
officer, whose rash orders led to several of his buddies being
killed in action. It sounded like something that could have and
should have been avoided. Although Robb was not great at
writing letters, after that incident, he wrote a lengthy letter to his
Senator. That impressed me. With all the time and
concentration he put into the effort, I knew it had to be most
important to him. It doesn't seem that it led to any good results
though.

Second letter from Robb in Washoe County jail, second week of June 1972:

"Mary, It really seems strange writing to you when you're only a couple of miles away, but then everything this past week has been very unreal, or very real, depending on how you look at it. You really looked beautiful Saturday, and I sure hope that it won't be years before we're together again. It looks that way though, so don't get your hopes up, because mine are preparing for the worst, which is probably what I'll get."

"Always remember that I love you. Love, Robb"

By then I had gotten a job at Harrah's hotel casino, and would have to come see him on my breaks, still in the blue uniform that we hotel desk clerks wore. These visits were short; they kept them to 15 minutes or so. It made me so sad to see him cooped up in a jail, when he loves the outdoors so much. I had a lot of fear about what could happen to him, and to us as a couple. So did he.

Letter from Robb from Washoe County jail, June 1972:

"Mary, Well, I'll tell you some of my feelings. I feel that I'm trapped in here with no control whatsoever over my environment, except my physical strength. I feel that I can lose you very easily to someone else, and I feel jealousy as I have never felt before. I never really liked to hear you talk about you and other guys, and I tried to limit my conversations on my past experiences. I do understand though and it doesn't bother me when I'm on the streets, but in here where there's nothing I can do about it, I feel terrible. You're all I have, Mary, and I knew that about a month after we broke up, years ago. I was too proud to go back then, and it was quite a while before I got over that. I want you to be mine forever and vice versa. If you could promise me that, I know I could make it through anything, and come out alright. If you can't, I'll understand. I like your ideas about life, and now that I'm being bombarded with religion, they

are the only things that keep my head straight. They're logical. I can see very easily how my brother changed so fast. He had to conform to my family's ideas or else have no real friends to turn to. I have you, Vogel and Brown, and he didn't. Vogel will always be my best friend, but you are that something that I need very much. I have never really given my love to anyone or anything, except myself, in my life. I had a girl friend that I came real close with but she moved to Phoenix and we kept our thing going for five years. It was her I saw in Vegas, and I'm sorry I lied. She still loved me, but her ideas on life and mine just didn't match up…. I need you and love you. Love, Robb"

This was the time when I started finding out who my real friends were…and weren't. That was a real eye-opening experience. Having people melt away out of my life, when I had done nothing wrong, was just another unfair situation, in my eyes. It seemed like this event was heaping one tragedy upon another on my young head. Now I'd be living all alone, covering the rent all by myself at the house we were planning to move into together. I'd given up going for a higher degree and my psyche was just too stunned to think about further studies at that point, anyway.

The future had suddenly become a blank slate and I had no idea what would be written on it now, or what to expect next. I knew that working for a big casino was not what I expected to do for the rest of my life.

From a very early age, I wanted to find something to do that would help other people. I give the credit for this inspiration to an older teacher who was substituting one day for my homeroom class back at Winnsboro High School in South Carolina. Miss Lily Lemon, I'm sure, was a relative as most people were in the little Irish/Scottish community in which I grew up, ten miles out in the country.

Miss Lemon looked around at all of us students and asked, *"Have you decided what you want to do to help the world yet?"* Oh my goodness, no! I had not, and didn't know until that very moment that I should be thinking about this. I felt embarrassed and inwardly humiliated that I had been so remiss in not thinking of this before. Of course, I was just 14 or 15 years old at that point, but still…one needs to plan ahead.

I have never forgotten her words, which remained as a dormant seed within me all those years at UNR pursuing a degree in a subject that I found interesting, but not something with which to profoundly change the world. If I would have made it to the Ph. D. program and later on to study in Africa, I'm sure it would have been interesting but it was not meant to be my path.

One of Robb's letters from Washoe County jail that summer touched on this quality he saw in me:

"….your ideas are good, Mary, and I know that you will do your best to save the world. You're way ahead of your time though, and most people are slow in catching up….always remember that I love you. Love, Robb"

Chapter Eight
Doing His Time in Prison
While I Did Mine, Alone at Home

R obb would often push me to move down to Lompoc, California, where the federal penitentiary was in which he was confined after his sentencing. It was a picturesque town, and I visited him several times, driving the long ten-hour trip with his parents. I didn't know anyone there and certainly had no job to go to or any sense of social connections in that place. My friends and some family members were in Reno. Why would he want to deprive me of that one bit of comfort I had left in my life?

Prior to his sentencing, I urged his attorneys to press for a brain scan to determine if his brain waves were normal. Well, they did that, and the test showed the brain activity was not normal, but the legal system was able to ignore that because *"they didn't have a pre-military service brain-wave test with which to compare it."* Oh, thank you very little.

His parents were staunchly into their Baptist religion, with a leaning way too fundamentalist for my taste. His dad refused to hire a good attorney for him, based on some type of punitive thinking that was along the lines of, *"If he did the crime, he should do the time,"* pay the price; repent of his sins and whatnot. I was taken aback by this attitude, but there was nothing I could do. This was long before the current day awareness of PTSD.

Robb ended up with two court-appointed attorneys. There was Coe Swobe, who at the time was also serving as a State Senator in the Nevada legislature, and a younger attorney, Keith Lee. It was Keith who later interviewed me, asking all the usual

39

questions – did I know anything about Robb's planning this act? *"Hell, no."* Well, I'm sure that I answered more politely than that, but that's what I was thinking and feeling.

Why does everyone always assume that the girlfriend is privy to every distorted thought in her man's brain? Oh yeah, and I just bet anything, that Robb knew in his gut that I would have pitched the biggest hissy fit ever, and thrown a monkey wrench into all his poorly laid plans, if he would have told me in advance. How could anyone believe that they could away with something as outrageous as skyjacking a passenger airliner? But he sure did believe he could get away with it at the time.

Then Keith Lee asked me if anyone else was involved, any accomplices? My reply was that I didn't think so, but how would I know about that, if I didn't even know this crime was afoot?

That interview was a walk in the park compared to the two FBI men showing up on my doorstep in what seemed like milliseconds after the event took place. How did they know that I was his girlfriend? How did they know where to find me, when I was just very temporarily staying at a friend's house? She had been packing boxes to move out of that place herself, so I'm sure all those boxes probably looked suspicious to the FBI agents. I was temporarily staying there, waiting for two other friends to vacate the small rental house that Robb and I planned to move into, up on 6th street, close to the university.

Thanks to my Celtic bloodline, I have always been rather intuitive and it's just gotten more developed and accurate, the older I get. I wish it had been working overtime prior to Robb taking the actions he did on June 2, 1972, but I really had no clue. He had done an excellent job of hiding it from me. I am quite sure that he instinctively knew that I would totally disapprove and raise the roof, telling him to ditch that plan.

In some of our early letters back and forth from the jail, I obviously wrote him that I wanted to beat him up. He wrote that he would have preferred that to where he was.

Letter from Robb from Washoe County jail, June 1972 – 1:30 a.m.:

"Mary, I just finished watching the late movie, and I have a hard time getting to sleep each night. It seems that every night I go over what will happen to me, and what will happen between you and me. I sure hope you get that chance to beat me up. To get bailed out for a few days, even a day, or a few hours, would mean so much to me. Today, or I guess yesterday, I won 3 candy bars, read half a book, and had my minister tell me that I was headed down the wrong path, and that my ideas on marriage and adultery will bring me more sorrow. He even made sense about some things. I only wish I knew where I was going, for how long, and that I could be with you. I love you, Robb"

He did not get bailed out, all that summer, and had to stay there in the county jail until his sentencing, when he was transferred to the Federal prison in Lompoc, California.

It seems to me jails and prisons are places that specialize in the death of the spirit. Recently there have been more inroads made in educational programs and even bringing meditation into prisons. That is what they need the most. In the "joint," as the convicts call it, every man or woman has to be an island unto himself or herself. There is a protective "shield," so to speak, around each one. It is a dangerous place to let any other inmates into the inner circle of one's heart as real friends. Robb had only me, as he often reminded me in those early days.

Letter from Robb from Washoe County jail, June or July 1972:

".... Just don't worry about me changing much in prison. People will change over periods of time, but you keep me informed on your ideas and what's happening, I'll read as much as I can, and I'll do alright. I've lived in a male protective shell most of my life. It's a good shell (one of the best), and it's got me through a lot of tough spots. I can harden my shell and survive, but I can always come out of it for you. You are one of the few people I've ever really let my real self be seen by. I've lived in a fake world all my life, and a couple more years won't change or bother me.

41

You stay around those clubs too long...and you'd better build yourself a shell, or take some low blows. I worry about you walking around like you do with all your defenses down. You seem to take care of yourself pretty well though, but I just have the feeling that you're walking a thin line sometimes. Write soon. Love, Robb"

Well, he was correct in that it was not my habit to walk through life putting up some big shield the way he had done to protect himself. It just wasn't in my nature. A shield? That sounds a lot like a wall to me. Walls are made to either keep people out, or keep people closed in. My goal is to have as much divine love flow through my heart as this human nervous system can handle and radiate that out to everyone. That's what makes the journey in this three-dimensional realm worth it to me. Walls and shields interfere with the free flow of this type of Higher Love. These were all things I realized some years later, once I was established on my spiritual path.

From my personal journal, dated September 5, 1972 (I did not ever show what I wrote to Robb, trying to save him from seeing the worst of my own despair – I was under the impression at this point, that it might take ten-years' time for him to get out on parole):

"Robb – We were so happy. And now part of me is gone, destroyed forever perhaps. Such a long ten years of our lives we were to share. I love you and my mind screams out in pain that I must no longer think of such happiness and pleasure and joy, at sharing all that's good in life. Sometimes I can't breathe. All this pain numbs my flesh and makes me small, meaningless. Empty fool with such ideas I used to share with you. This can't be right. Our separation is too cruel to bear. Can the years leave us the same as we were – 22. Don't they know; can't they see – some of me is dead, dead, dead. I can no longer be light. Seldom laugh. Often cry in agony – alone. For Christ sake, did Voltaire have the truth?"

Well, I cannot recall which Voltaire quote I was referring to then, but I'm sure it was a good one. At UNR, I had taken a Women's Studies Honors class, and I was very involved with the Women's Liberation Movement of the day. Of course, I had tried to educate Robb and share with him all I had learned and observed in these studies. In another letter from Robb, from Washoe County Jail, after one of my weekly visits to him there, he wrote:

"....I want you to know that every TV program, commercial, or any wisecrack about women in here reminds me of everything you've taught me. It's like being on a weird drug that lets you see everything differently, and in its true form. I guess it's knowledge that a person can't lose or forget for the rest of his or her life. You just have faith in me and I'll make you proud of me. Please. You looked so beautiful today. I love and miss you, honey. Love, Robb

Yes, I did believe in Robb. I had faith in his innate goodness and ability to keep it together even in the challenging environment of prison life. The hardest part was in not knowing how many years of separation we were really looking at back then. That was the big unknown.

Chapter Nine
A Time to Grow:
Sharing Our Feelings in Letters

S ome spiritual writers describe how our "far memory" is shut off when we are born so that most people don't consciously remember any past lives. Otherwise, it is like "taking an open book test." What would be the point of that?

It is the spiritual growth we achieve by a lot of work on ourselves, especially when such so-called unplanned and traumatic events occur, that is where we prove our mettle here in Earth School.

One of the biggest compliments I've ever received came in recent years, from my good friend Sandra in Boulder, Colorado. She said, *"Mary, you are one who LIVES your spirituality."* Well, thank you so much – I do try. Considering where I came from, there has been a far distance to travel. Sometimes we are blessed to have comrades-at-arms to help lighten the emotional load with their companionship; there are other tests that we have to face totally alone.

Alone is how it felt to me in the days after I learned the news from his sister that Robb had done this audacious act. It was such a stone-cold solitary time, with no one to turn to. Back then, I had not developed the awareness that we are always surrounded by our guardian angels, and thus never really alone. I can't even remember how long it took me to call my parents and tell them. They may have learned about it from my aunt. It's not that I felt ashamed of Robb. I was trying to understand the pressures he must have been under to even think of attempting such a thing. Others in my family probably felt embarrassed. As

I said, certain "friends" began to shun me and disappear from my life.

Some of those early letters from the Reno jail seemed to show that he'd come to appreciate much of the knowledge that I had acquired and had been sharing with him. In one letter from Washoe County jail, he wrote:

"....You do know a lot. Maybe more than I can comprehend. Those four years were not wasted by you as they were by me. I will try and catch up, and I hope you'll help me. I wish that I could talk to you about a lot of things that I'm thinking about. I did learn something in those four years, if by only accident and experience alone. I might be able to give you some advice on your friends, and then I might not. I know that women have closer and more lasting friendships (on the average) than men. I know from experience that friends are not as close to you as they appear to be. In war and jail it's easy to see friends in a true light, and draw lines. You don't have that chance, so that's about all I can say. I also know that about the best friends a person has are his parents, even if they are several gaps apart. My grandmother told me that years ago when she said that they will always be there and stick with you, and if your parents aren't your friends, then you don't have many. I can see that in jail. Some of these people don't have their parents as friends, and they don't have any (real friends). Don't let your friends upset you. A real friend knows how his friend thinks, and knows what he wants and how to help him when needed. They'll come to you. Try not calling them all the time and starting the action and maybe you'll see them in a true light. Quit making excuses up for them on why they won't do something. Out of those four girls, you're doing quite well if one is a true friend. I don't know what's happening out there though. You know your friends and I don't, so good luck. I can say one thing for sure. I'm your friend and I love you, Robb"

Later that summer some of the inmates at Washoe County jail in Reno attempted a jailbreak, but Robb did not participate. It made me feel very good that I was playing the role of "conscience" within his mind now, and he decided to listen to that voice, rather than join the troublemakers. He describes this in another letter from jail:

"Mary, I guess you heard about that attempted jailbreak out of here early Sunday morning. It was out of my dorm, and I didn't go. That's all I can tell you about it till I see you next. I had a real hard time making the decision to stay. If you would have been here to talk to me, you probably would have told me to stay, so I just imagined that you were here, and listened to you...."

Certainly there were some days that I couldn't hide how down I was feeling and he was sensitive enough to see that. There are some comments in a couple of his letters home from Washoe County jail that reflect a lot about how we were both feeling at the time:

"....For some reason you looked very depressed yesterday. I wish that there was something that I could do to make you feel better. I don't want you reading those books like the 'Glass House' and worrying about me. If there is one thing that I can assure you of, it is that I can take care of myself, and in most cases, get over. I realize what I'm getting into. I'll have to play all kinds of games (as they're called in here)...and probably get in a few fights. Federal pens are the best though, and you really don't have to worry about me. I can tell that the idea of us being apart is getting more real each day. It is for me. I just want you to know that I want to hold you, kiss you, and be near you as much as I did two months ago. I just plain love you and there's no getting it out of my mind, and I'm not trying. Your mind is beautiful, but don't ever think that I bypassed your long hair, nice body, cute face in summing up your beauty. I love it all and miss you. Love, Robb"

He was referring to Truman Capote's book *The Glass House*, which was made into a movie with Alan Alda. Sure, I was concerned that even if I was able to wait for him, he might come out so warped by the years in prison, that I might not even recognize who he was by then. It did feel great though, to receive all those reassurances of his love for me.

I so wish we had all known about PTSD back then. Looking at one of his letters from Washoe County jail that summer of 1972, I can now see the evidence of it, but we did not know a name for this syndrome at that time. If only we had known; if only we could have used knowledge of this condition to try to get a more lenient sentence for him. Robb wrote:

"Mary, I'm still reading a lot and find myself falling into a trap. I take what I learn and try to analyze all kinds of things. It's a very painful process sometimes. I must find a way to enjoy what I learn, and make it useful and not harmful. Maybe you don't understand what I just said so I'll put it a different way. I've found so little enjoyment in the last couple of years (not counting loving you) that I enjoy a lot of simple things, like watching 'All in the Family,' because it makes me laugh…. I've learned enough from books since I've been in here to see now that you gave me a lot of slack, and I've learned enough about life while in here to see that you gave me some slack there too. Why? Please continue to do so, ok?…. It does seem like such a long time until we will be together again, and it does all seem so very unreal. I'm no criminal, and I keep thinking that I'll wake up and it will all be a terrible nightmare. The only bright side of the whole thing is my finishing college, and that isn't a very bright side. I miss you so much, and the thought of being away from you is worse than the idea of going to prison. Some day everything will be beautiful again. All my love, Robb"

The next letter from Robb has some more accurate reflections of how I was feeling, especially the "unlucky in love" part:

"...I think your friends are good people, even though some of them have a lot more hang-ups than they think they have.... You might think yourself unlucky in love, life and friendships, but you'll get your return twice fold some day, and I want to be there.... I want you to know that I really care about what you want out of life, and that it does matter what you do. I don't want you getting stoned all the time. Sometimes you can be so smart, and at other times so (I can't think of the word). I feel, and have felt, like a little child under your arms at times, and at other times I feel like I should, and have to lead you. 'Mary can be a super woman if she wants to.' It's all up to you, and that's about all I or anyone can say. I wish I was out there to enjoy your life with you. I can enjoy life wherever I go, and it puzzles me sometimes, that other people can't be like that. I miss you though, like I've never missed before, so I guess I love you and I guess I always will. What is love? (find me a good descriptive poem, please) Miss you so much, Robb p.s. how's my spelling coming along?"

In one letter from Robb from Washoe County jail that summer of 1972, he spoke of "going on a campaign against his own ignorance," with a plan of doing a lot of reading. He mentions *"...everything I've read on various topics supports what you say."* In that same letter he wrote:

"Mary, I'm sorry to hear about your friends splitting up.... I just wish I was out there to help you through all this. Together we could do anything in the world, and no one could hurt us. You just don't know how sorry I am that I screwed up, or how many times I've wished that I could go back in time to that day. Just keep your head together and remember that I love you.... Keep your hopes up, and keep those cards, letters, articles and books coming in. I'm going to learn all I can. All my love, Robb p.s. I'm sorry that I'm not the most romantic person in the world, and I seem to be a failure at writing down what I really want to say

and get across to you. Just remember that if I could, I would, and I'll try because I do love you."

Letter from Robb in the Washoe County jail, Reno, NV approximately August 21, 1972:

"Honey, In the beginning of this crime I knew I could do it, and get away free. I thought the money would give me security for the rest of our lives. It also would give me some pride in knowing that I'd finally done something. You, more than anyone, know how weak I really am, and up until now I've done nothing but try and prove myself to myself. I realized before I took the plane that the money would not give me security. Only love can do that. It was the idea that I knew I could do it, and the eternal fight to prove myself that made me go through with it. I see now that I couldn't do it and I proved very little to myself. It proved one thing to me though. I see that I'm not so smart, that I really love you, and that crime is no way to seek for what one wants…. Very little that I've done in my life has turned out good…. I don't want to feel that all my life efforts were in vain. The only thing I ever did right was fall in love with you. Now I'm going to do time, and I know it won't be a dream land for us. I don't know much about love, or how long it lasts, or if you'll fall in love with someone else. I do know that I can do the time, and come out loving you, and I know that I need you more than anything else to help me. If you do find someone else, I want you to please continue to help me. You are my contact with the way of life I want to live, and I'll believe what you say. I want to see you, hold you, and talk to you about all these things so much. I really look forward to a visit from you when I get to where I'm going. While I'm in jail I'll learn as much as I can, and we could live happily ever after….I LOVE YOU. Your true lover, Robb"

Wouldn't that request for help melt even the hardest heart? I took that responsibility to help him seriously. His spirit and sense of hope was not going to die "on my watch." I would "have his back" as best I could. I had stuck by him through his Vietnam Army days and I would try and be there for him through his long prison term. Many times, I would worry about my own future, too.

There were issues for me to deal with that Robb could not even take the time to think of, I'm sure, as he had to get a bearing on his new surroundings and determine his approach and persona that he'd have to mold to be okay in prison. At least he could go outside in the prison yard once he was moved to Lompoc, and feel some sunshine on his skin and fresh air on his face there versus the stifling confines of the Washoe County jail where he had to stay all summer long, until his sentencing.

Just prior to his sentencing that August, Robb wrote a poem, that he sent me from Washoe County jail:

"The Sun shines through the windows, casts shadows on the wall. My hopes and fears have buried each other, other feelings and senses aren't here at all. Everything is as calm as death, though I'm alive, I feel small. Knowledge, love, peace, truth, and you are waiting, and I hear your call. Calm is today, but calmer still, is the wish to have them all."

His sentencing was on August 25, 1972, and Judge Thompson handed him a 30-year sentence. In any event, it was a merciful gesture that the judge sent him to Lompoc Federal Penitentiary in California rather than some of the worse prisons in the land, which house more hardcore criminals. This place was known for its prison population being more the white-collar crime type of offenders. Robb certainly met and hung out with some interesting characters, including H. R. Haldeman, serving time for his role in the Watergate break-in, with whom he played bridge at times.

There was still a lot of boredom to contend with and he wrote that the nights were the worst time of all.

Well, there was not much I could do about that, and his pain at being confined was mirrored in my frustration that he had done something to put himself there, in the first place. No doubt, my frustration, impatience, or irritation must have shown through the lines in some of my letters. He complimented me for giving him a lot of slack, but sometimes he'd get a little defensive about something I'd said or the way he took it.

I was much more impatient when I was younger. It is true what they say about age mellowing people. Thank heavens. That is one good thing about aging, anyway.

It was not in my power to free him from his prison. All I could do was keep his mind going with stimulating ideas, sharing books and sending him magazine subscriptions. Then we would write back and forth about the books after he read them. I sent him subscriptions to *Psychology Today* and *MS. Magazine*, which he was open-minded enough to actually read. Later he asked for a *Playboy* subscription as a consolation prize for having to read *MS.* for a year. As if that was going to happen!

This enforced separation was hard on us both. Our only interaction then was the letters we wrote to one another. At times, we would bicker a little, with me playing the spelling cop and grammar nazi on him. His spelling errors really did drive me crazy. It was just one of my pet peeves, and I insisted that he get a dictionary. One of his letters from prison was pretty funny on the subject. Reading through my notebook of all his letters from jail and prison which I've saved since 1972, certainly has reminded me of Robb's good sense of humor and even made me laugh aloud at times. Going through these letters and finding these funny passages, has been like revisiting special old conversations. The laughing has been a real tonic for me, through some tears.

Letter from Robb dated October 15, 1972, from Lompoc prison:

"Hey, If I misspell those again (he was forever spelling it "thoes," which drove me nuts) *just count to ten, cuss out loud, and then learn to spell it my way. You might also ponder over the word and ask yourself if I did it on purpose or accidentally. Among all*

the other misspelled words though, it would hardly be noticeable. I still don't have my dictionary, but will soon. Please be patient, for you will soon be reading my letters clearly, and rejoicing. Thank you...."

In one of my letters to him, it seems that I mentioned his previous letter sounded too distant. Responding to this point in his letter of November 16, 1972, he addressed his own emotional nature: *"....Sorry if that one letter seemed cold or logical. I am very emotional, and I love the softness in me, too. If I try to be hard, I can't. I forgive you for all the mistakes made, and I know mine are really big mistakes. You know something that I've thought about. We are both pretty weak people, but we're better off half the time than other people, and better all the time when we're together. You always talked like you had the answer to everything, and you never said that my point of view was ever right (except when it was similar to yours.) You still don't, but sometimes I get the feeling that something I said would make you think. You always made me think. More thoughts. I think that you have had a pretty rough life up to now, and you've done alright for yourself. You seem to have this battle against you and yourself going all the time, and I don't like the results sometimes. Example: instead of saying the job opportunities aren't probably that good down here, etc., etc., and rather than moving down, you have to get yourself together up in Reno, so I don't think I'll move down, and saying I just wish I could hold you, I love you so much, wish I was there and if you didn't love me, I don't know what I'd do in your letter. I know that getting yourself together one way or the other has little or nothing to do with your moving down here. I know that there are more people and jobs within 150 miles of this place than Nevada ever hoped to see. I know you don't have a car, don't have much money, and don't want to leave the friends you have. I don't expect you to move down here, and I think you've put yourself out visiting me twice. I enjoy the visits, and do wish I could see you more often, but that's the way things go sometimes. To sum it all up. Sometimes you say what you don't really mean, but then this letter is no masterpiece, but you can probably see that I'm troubled about something. I can't pinpoint it in writing, but I assure you it's trivial. After reading this letter up to this point I realize that my writing isn't worth a _____. I will get better, and I sure as hell get tired of writing I-love-you letters. You know I love you. Right? So I have to say something, and that means bothering you about things you say that I think about. I realize that we're people, and make mistakes. I realize that if you started getting on my case and telling me my faults, that it would be a year before I got the completed letter. I just don't have anything better to do, so I think of how things could be better for us. I love you. Robb"*

Ah, there was his delightful humor again, shining through his stress and worry, making me laugh. I sure missed laughing with Robb, and yes, holding him, too…all the things he wanted me to gush over, but that was just too painful to keep doing, not knowing how long we would be apart.

I was glad that Robb was taking courses and learning as much as he could while in prison, and I tried to be supportive of his endeavors. He started to worry about us "drifting apart" and expressed his feelings in a letter dated November 22, 1972:

"…. I get a feeling that jail brought us closer together, but that now we are slowly drifting apart. I don't want it that way. I still love and miss you very much, but I guess that's the way things go. I want to see you again soon. You can talk about how bad things are out there and make me feel a little better, but the truth is that I'm in prison and hey, I really do need you now. Not when I get out or when you get yourself together, but now, while I'm in here. I don't really have the right to ask anything of you, but I need someone real to talk to. It's not like the Army. There's people in the Army to talk to and good times. Letters are nice, but they are just paper with a few thoughts. I know how you feel about coming down here and you're right. This is just what I feel

and need, and whenever you get a chance to make it down here for a visit, do. Love, Robb"

In one letter that Robb sent me from Lompoc prison in late November, 1972, he included a drawing he had made. This picture really spoke volumes and gets back to the question of *"Why did he do it?"* It shows fields in the distance with Vietnamese people in traditional clothing and hats to block the Sun, laboring in their rice fields. There's the military outpost at which he was stationed and a guard tower with a machine gun on it. Then he depicts the bunkers in which the soldiers were staying. He must have been talking to a fellow soldier here. The conversation went like this, with someone asking him, *"What'll you do when you get home?"* His answer was, *"I think I'll skyjack an airplane."* His buddy's response was, *"You'll get caught and go to jail."* Robb's answer: *"Maybe so, and maybe not, but either way I'll have done something in life that will let America know I'm alive and kicking."* The buddy then says, *"If you make it no one will know you did it."* His final comment is, *"They'll know someone did it, and I'll have inner peace forever."*

Gee, what a clear demonstration, from my perspective, of PTSD at work. His letter accompanying this drawing, dated November 29, 1972, throws further light on his state of mind. *"There is no inner peace in skyjacking a plane, true, but there is some personal fulfillment there. You don't see it, and I can't put my finger on it, but in a world with so many people, countless names, and very little personal recognition, I let people out there know that I was around and that any fool can stand out in a crowd. I couldn't see writing a book about it, because it has no meaning and relates to nothing more than a few people's personal lives. I would like to write something that people could enjoy, relate to, and learn from...."*

To me, a lot of his thinking here reflected the definition of alienation and anomie that I had so recently been studying in my sociology classes at UNR.

He went on to include some personal feelings about our relationship that were on his mind at that time, *"Now to you and me. I do need you now and you know that. I do love you, but it makes me feel secure in no way at all. I feel at your mercy.... When I think of all the good things we had, and how I can use your love to better myself in so many ways, I know I'll want you when I get out, and forever if I can fix it. I have no intention of using you or anyone else. I want us to stay as close to each other as we can, and I want to plan for a future that is for us and not me, myself and I. I have lots of interesting ideas that I'll tell you about when we meet, and I have all kinds of hopes, dreams.... Hey, I can do it all and make it come true, all I need is you. If you can stay with me, and I'm not saying that's going to be easy for you, I'm yours. All my love, Robb"*

Much later, in a letter from Lompoc prison dated September 24, 1973, he wrote:

"I miss you and love you, and I had a weird dream the other night that let me know that I will be out some day and see you again. Love, Robb"

That turned out to be a prophetic dream, but we could not know that at the time. It was going to take quite a few years to come true.

Life magazine had a photo of Robb and all the other failed skyjackers of the year in its very last issue, December 29, 1972. I have saved a copy of that all these years, too. It didn't look like him, with that glum and sullen expression. It was a picture of a man caught doing something he was sure he'd be successful doing, and who could hardly believe he had been caught. It was a picture of more than that to me. Not only was it the man I loved, but it was the embodiment of every veteran who did not get any counseling when they returned from the war – any war. *"When will they ever learn, when will they ever learn?"* as the old folk song goes.

Chapter Ten

A Road Less Traveled:
My Spiritual Path Begins

I stayed in touch with Robb for three years and traveled the distance to see him at least three times, with his parents. In one of his letters from Lompoc, dated April 19, 1973, he thanked me for coming to see him: *"Sorry I haven't written sooner. I really enjoyed that last visit, but what I really enjoy is the inspiration you give me. It is so reassuring to know that you are really real, and there...."*

However, I started getting interested in a more spiritual way of life, and there wasn't any way to share that with Robb while he was still locked up. I did write to him about the books that I was reading, and all that I was learning.

David, on the other hand, distant and cool as ice, was someone I could never quite forget. In 1968, he learned meditation and his partying way of life came to a quick end. Then he was on a campaign to get me, and everyone else he knew, on the meditation bandwagon. I resisted for five years because of how cold he was to me. I wanted his love and he only wanted to be a preachy Mr. Know-It-All. Darn it.

Before we knew it, he had to do his military service and be off to Vietnam. He resented the heck out that, and felt he was *"the only meditator he knew who had to go to Nam."* Yes, well if you could see those photos in uniform that he later shared with me – wow, what war does to men's psyche is a real crime against Nature.

When he finally got home, we saw each other. With David and me, it was rather like one of those "same time, next year" scenarios. I think one time in his military service years there was a two-year gap between seeing him. I felt such an intense connection to him, and felt hurt by his emotional rejections. This was to be a case of "unrequited love" for me, from the get-go. Only many years later would I learn what the definition and qualities of a narcissist were. It's sad to think that someone so intelligent and so spiritual could also be afflicted with that condition.

I can recall borrowing my aunt's 1964 Mustang and driving the distance to Carson City to see David, sometimes unannounced. I knew I wasn't likely to run into him being with any other woman, recluse that he was. He was generally happy to see me, and sometimes it would be him calling me up, to get together. What I felt for him was a strange but mystical connection that would not quit. There was some kind of fascination for me, as his mind was always off on philosophical topics in true visionary style.

About a year after Robb got home from Vietnam and in short order, skyjacked that United Flight, David was visiting my cousin and saw me. He said, *"I hear one of your boyfriends had to go to prison for skyjacking that plane from the Reno airport."* Yes, that's true. This time his urging me to learn meditation worked.

It was a good thirteen months after Robb's crime that I finally let David talk me into learning Transcendental Meditation. I was initiated into the TM practice on July 28, 1973. Of course, from that first experience, I regretted not learning five years earlier, when he first pushed me to do it, but I wasn't going to let him know that. I still had my pride.

This was the life-changing break that I needed. I had a teacher and I was gaining a huge amount of spiritual knowledge day-by-day and week-by-week as I plunged into an overdue overhaul of my thinking. Thank heavens for spiritual teachers and their willingness to help us transcend the barriers of our own ignorance.

From the very beginning, when I directly experienced in my very first meditation "this really works," I started saving the funds for my TM teacher training course, which would be held in Europe. I had never traveled abroad before. Of course, my security-oriented parents were fretting, sending me articles of how some members of some cult got stranded in a foreign country when their leader took their plane tickets home away, or their passports, or some such malarkey. No one would ever get their hands on any ticket home of mine. My mother didn't raise a fool, as the old saying goes. I may have been young and still fairly naïve, but not an idiot.

Meditation teacher training remains one of the highlights of my life, as it does for most of my fellow participants. There is just nothing like this meditation to melt away layers of stress and ignorance, from my experience. All that I was learning was going to help many people, once I got back home and became an active teacher in the field, so that is what I was committed to. Finally, I could face my now internalized Miss Lily Lemon with my head held high.

I had to quit smoking pot or taking any other type of drug as a standard prerequisite for taking this four-day meditation course. Everyone is told prior to initiation that drugs prevent the mind from transcending; even marijuana does that. That was easy for me. I just made a commitment and kept it. Well, that changed my life in the most positive ways imaginable. I never had a desire for any of that stuff from the first day that I started to meditate. So once again, I had to admit that David was right. That part wasn't fun for my ego, but what was I to do, but meditate twice a day and enjoy the results.

Who knows? Without the blessings of inner peace, which my new meditation practice brought me, with the weight of so much pain, loss, and depression pulling me down, I could have ended up as an alcoholic, drug addict, or worse – perhaps lost in a sea of self-pity, which is one of the worst poisons for the soul. So I had many things for which to thank David.

Actually, it was "Lord Dave" who got me interested in anthropology in the first place. Soon after I met him, we were talking a walk one time in an old graveyard in my aunt and uncle's neighborhood. He was fascinated with history and could talk at length about it (or any other subject). Then we went back to my aunt's Ford Mustang where we'd parked it and tried making love in the back seat. A Mustang is not a very comfortable vehicle for such activity, I must say.

I think David and I only had perhaps seven romantic interludes in the eight years after I first met him, but being with him was always memorable to me. I don't mean in a sexual way. We were kids fumbling around, not knowing what we were doing anyway. Years later, as friends, he would tell me, "*I have no complaints,*" as to those experiences. Fine, but it was all on a much deeper, soul-connection level for me.

One night some time after I learned to meditate, I felt so drawn to go visit him in Carson City; I again borrowed my aunt's car and went to find him. He had me sit in his lap and I was trying to tell him, *"I know that I've known you before."* I was just learning about reincarnation, which was a thrilling new discovery and deep explanation of cause and effect for me. If ever I had had a past life with anyone, it had to be THIS man. We then went to his bedroom and while we were making love, I couldn't help but say that again, wondering where I had known him before. It was more like an inner knowing that this was true rather than a question. He laughingly made some smart-ass joke*: "Oh, should I put on a Trojan helmet or something?" (Well no, but how about just a Trojan?)* Ha, ha.

My meditation teacher turned me on to a lady in Pacific Palisades, California who was good at getting into the Akashic Records to see these past lives. Her name was Ethlyn Luce. I just had to find out about the David connection and about Robb, and which one of these men I should marry this time...if there was even going to be a choice about that.

She was quite good at her work and the spiritual wisdom that poured forth was very helpful. She said that it is more important to be careful with the "how" of your Being than the "who, why, when, where" and all of that. She also spoke of the mighty power of Forgiveness, which is a bigger force on this planet, more cleansing and healing than we can even imagine. If we manage the "how" of our Being, a Higher Force will take care of all the rest. That spiritual insight was to serve me well as time went on.

What I learned in that reading was that in ancient Egypt David and I had been married. He was a philosopher and I was an alchemist. She said perhaps there was a need for more emotional connection in this life. Oh, so I guess that he was Mister Too Cerebral even back in that lifetime, too. Wouldn't you know?

As to Robb, we were young and in love, living in the South, when the Civil War broke out in the lifetime just before this current incarnation. His name was Jonathon Dover and he was a soldier in that war. I was supposedly Mary Jane Appleby, the daughter of a plantation owner in South Carolina. I've never taken the time to research that family from back in those days, but it certainly would be an interesting study. Robb, or Jonathon then, and I were engaged to be married. He got killed in the war, and it broke my heart. I actually went into a convent, she said, and surrounded myself with beautiful things. No wonder his being put away for maybe decades in prison in this life, felt like going through another major death-like loss experience to me now.

Of course, Robb would have none of this. He called her a fortune teller and a "majic (sic) lady." I wrote him all about that reading, as I told him everything. We were always so honest with each other, probably to my own detriment.

He wrote me early in February 1974, saying, *"I do feel you're right in saying we planned this whole thing. I just hope everything works out alright. I love you, Robb."* On February 15, 1974, he wrote showing much interest in learning what my reading with Ethlyn Luce "the majic lady" revealed. In referring to the reading he wrote, *"If you weren't a man in your past life (most recent), the tape's a phony."* Okay, Robb, what's that supposed to mean? I hope it was a compliment.

I transcribed that tape of the past-life reading, and sent him a printed copy of it, along with a birthday card in early March of 1974. He responded on March 11, 1974. Here's an excerpt of that letter:

"Mary, ...I can't say I believe in reincarnation or not, but I don't think that tape is the truth. It just sounded like a bunch of astrology philosophy mixed with some mumbo jumbo crap that didn't really tell you anything. I'm probably wrong like I have been most of my life, but I just can't get into that. You obviously believe that tape, so I will make believe I do too, and write this letter. If I died in some war then I have probably lived another life since then, and obtained some kind of karmic carryover. I thought for a while that this prison stuff might be some kind of lesson or something, but it in no way enables a person to improve his life or soul. I must be moving downhill. I also saw that you were deciding between two people for a partner in life. I can help you out there, because I am the worst choice by far. I will probably be here another five years, and like I said, I'm heading downhill. I think like a criminal. I think we've cleared up any karmic obligations, and exchanged ideas. David – seems to be more in tune with your thoughts so you'd fare a lot better. Who's to say I won't jump from girl to girl when I get out. I always did before, and probably won't change a bit. I don't like to write this stuff because you are pretty important to me, but you should be happy and I can never give you that forever.... You might not even care about David, but what I say applies to anyone you might meet in the next five years.

"Back to me being a non-believer. I am a man of little faith (a hard case). My parents don't seem to reach me with their religious stuff, and your chances are similar with the magic lady material. I still love you and like hearing from you though. So let me know how things work out. Love, Robb"

His tough-guy talk didn't fool me. He just didn't want to put me through more of the emotional agony of waiting for him any longer, for an unknown number of years. Our karma was far from over, as it turned out, as we would both find out later.

Chapter Eleven
Deeper Spiritual Knowledge
Helps Light My Way

I was certainly not out looking for a new man to love, because I still loved Robb and wanted to be there for him. One evening, a guy friend of the previous occupants stopped by at my rented house on 6th Street; he was looking for Frances and Nickie but stuck around to chat with me. Upon hearing my story, he decided that what I really needed was sex with him to ease my grief. I promptly showed him to the door. Is that all these guys THINK about? Sheesh, Good riddance to him.

I needed some new friends and the best one I was to meet was Loretta (we called her Rhetta) who had long, beautiful red hair and worked with me at Harrah's Hotel Casino. She had a kind and gentle heart, and such a genuine spiritual depth, that we became fast friends. It was a blessing to share spiritual ideas and understanding in our many conversations.

There was one evening that David called and wanted to come see me. I actually made dinner for him that night. It had to be vegetarian, per his dietary preferences. I remember curried rice being one of the dishes I made and he sure ate it up. I am ashamed to admit I did put some beef bouillon in the dish, as that is what the recipe called for. Well, I hadn't learned to be a vegetarian cook at that point. He never knew the difference. He probably would have "had a cow" if he had known.

After dinner, I shared that tape of my Ethlyn Luce past life reading and he sat there with his eyes closed listening to it. He had had a session with her himself, so he knew that her work was good. He told me about his reading, and I noted that he certainly didn't ask any questions about me in it. I was wearing a long yellow dress that night. He seemed to find it attractive.

I know he was both intrigued and intimidated when he heard Ethlyn answering my question, *"Which of these two men should I marry?"* He made some comment about it afterwards but didn't have the nerve to go deeply into the subject. When he was leaving, he said that this was really the last time we should see each other in any capacity other than friendship. He had done everything he could; it seemed to me, to squash his own passionate sexuality. Man, what a waste; well, that was my point of view. I wondered if he'd made some vow to God, that if he could just make it home safely from Vietnam, he would then follow the straight and narrow path and become a spiritual celibate. An intuitive reader years later confirmed this probability to me. That is certainly how his life was turning out to be, and ultimately, he never married or even lived with anyone. He chose a monk-like path. I guess that maybe it had to do with the energetic reality that until someone really learns to love himself; he is not able to accept love that wants to come to him from anyone else...nor give it to anyone else.

Later I went to see a local psychic in Reno who was devoted to Padre Pio and only used the Bible in her readings. After praying she opened the Bible, her fingers went down the page and she suddenly stopped. She looked up at me and asked, *"Who is David?"* Oh geez, how could she know that? She also mentioned something about me wearing a yellow dress, so I guess she saw that, too. I don't recall what advice she gave me, but no advice was going to work when it came to getting David interested in possibly having a life with me. That was just the way it was and one of those "this is what is" things I had to accept and come to terms with. Well, sort of. I tried. But, he would still pop up in my mind from time to time through the years.

Unrequited or impossible love seemed to be the name of the game for me. It just didn't seem fair; one in jail and one living like a monk in his own internal world down in Carson City. Why me, oh Lord? There are some mysteries for which there are just no answers while we are in this worldly life.

I do believe that everything happens for a reason. Robb had things to learn about life that he probably never would have, left to his own devices in the outside world, with his "outer stroke" activities-based focus. He puts that pretty well himself in one letter to me.

Portions of a letter from Robb, November 8, 1972, Lompoc prison:

*"Mary, It's good to hear that you're getting it together....thank those people for praying for me, and tell them honestly with a straight face that if it weren't for God I know I wouldn't be here, and that I thank him every day. Tell them that he wouldn't do anything that wasn't for my own good. Ok. I kind of wish that he'd stop being so good to me. It is good for my head to be here though. I have to admit that it has helped me get myself together....*He then mentions taking some finals for courses he was enrolled in, and he had gotten a good grade on his term paper in American history, noting that his teacher said: *"...it was the best one he's ever seen come out of this place. I now have in my locker a dictionary. It's blue in color and has every word spelled perfectly. We'll see if it helps."* There he goes again, trying to make me laugh, which I did appreciate. He wrote these words at the top of this letter: *"You may be at a worse place, but I'm behind bars."*

It would be so nice if I had copies of the letters I wrote to him, but I didn't think to make copies of them back then. I'm sure I would laugh at some of my own language and ways of thinking then, were I to see them now. We were both doing the best we could with a very trying situation. It was a good thing to see that most of the time Robb was able to keep his sense of humor, though as he said, the nights were harder. I'm sure he had many thoughts of me while he was sleeping alone in that cold, lonely jail cell.

Sometimes you just love someone, no matter if there's a different point of view or focus about what's important in life. I know we were both loving and respectful to each other when we were a couple, and now I can appreciate the special connection we shared back then though we were both so uncomfortable with this forced separation.

There wasn't much else for me to do but go inward, more into my spiritual path. At least I knew that this was something that was helping me, while also giving me the ability to help others and contribute to world peace. That was certainly a better focus than running around all over town "looking for love in all the wrong places." I was too discriminating to go down that path, but I sure was lonely. I guess I mentioned that to Robb a lot in my letters, too. Sometimes he would respond to those comments, but I didn't get the feeling that he was able to put himself in my shoes, and imagine what I was going through, feeling so alone and lost without him by my side, out in the world by myself. There are different types of "prisons" that we humans can experience, and not all of them have visible bars.

Not knowing if he would have a chance to get out of prison before the full 30-year sentence, it's not like we could plan "a life together" any more. We didn't know what was going to happen. In the following six years, I did briefly date four guys, but nothing serious at all. Of course, there was the very rare encounter with David, too.

At least David and I could now talk on the same playing field, since I'd learned to meditate, and attended lectures by his favorite teacher as well, Charlie Lutes. I certainly felt that my spiritual knowledge had caught up with his, after graduating from my international TM teacher-training course in Europe. I think all that did was make him more afraid of me than ever. Was I getting a little too close spiritually and intellectually for his ego's comfort?

It was so obvious that we had this deep connection from the day I met him at the tender age of 16. Why couldn't he just admit it, even to himself? That was one more grand disappointment for me in the journey of this life. I know he thought of me as "good people" as he would tell mutual friends years later, but …I guess his path was not to be one that included a "partner" in Earth School class this time. It has always amazed me that I could feel something, some soul recognition for someone, so very deeply, and not have it reciprocated.

Our meditation program founder mentioned that men have denser nervous systems than women do. I guess there is a purpose to that. Traditionally, men do more of the hard, physical labor, which requires more strength than most women have. Women, being the child bearers of the species, have a more refined nervous system, and thus more sensitivity (it certainly does seem) to be the nurturers of the young in society, and the ones to care about feelings more, keeping that emotional energetic structure of community alive.

When we were very young and still in the grass-smoking days, David would tease me that some day I'd end up a "house frau" (housewife) and be one of the "carriers of the species." Oh, bless his little detached Aquarius Moon heart. Grrr, he really had a way of getting to me and pushing my buttons, which I guess showed he had some interest at least.

Such are the concerns of a teenager. Now, at age 22, I had bigger concerns, and I didn't feel a whole lot of power to do much about them. At least I could get a job, so I did that. I walked downtown to my Harrah's hotel-casino job, until I could manage getting a loan for a little used car. It certainly was not the vehicle to try to take on long trips. Visiting Robb would have to remain by courtesy of his parents taking me with them when they went to see him in Lompoc, California. I know that it made Robb's day, so to speak, on those rare occasions when I did get there, and he wanted to see me more than that, but this is all I could swing.

My life was beginning to feel like "nowhere to go but up" in the spiritual sense of the word. The two men I had loved while in high school and then college, were unavailable or unobtainable, for such different reasons. I could not see too far into my own future then, and felt disempowered to make much happen on the relative level of life, so I stuck with my quiet, meditative lifestyle. Robb summed it up in one of his letters, which I shared earlier, that maybe I was feeling "unlucky in love." Yeah, no kidding.

Well, though I tried to fight it, there were certainly times in which I felt more than unlucky. Was I cursed to walk through this life all alone? Some of my journal entries showed a lot of this frustration, despair, and depression. It was a rather deep hole to dig out of, and meditation is the one powerful tool that got me out of it.

Many of my journal entries of that period indicate what I was going through then. There were also many uplifting quotes I included in them, to help lift myself out of the heaviness of the times. Here are some prime examples:

"In the mountains of truth you never climb in vain."
— Friedrich Nietzsche

"Who can doubt that we exist only to love? We live not a moment exempt from its influence."
— Blaise Pascal

"Far away there in the sunshine are my highest aspirations. I may not reach them, but I can look up and see their beauty, believe in them, and try to follow where they lead." – Louisa May Alcott

"Only that day dawns to which we are awake."
— Henry David Thoreau

"…It is only important to love the world…to regard the world and ourselves and all beings with love, admiration and respect." – Hermann Hesse

"To know someone here or there with whom you can feel there is understanding in spite of distances or thoughts unexpressed – that can make of this earth a garden." – Johann Wolfgang von Goethe

"In the midst of winter, I finally learned that there was in me an invincible summer." – Albert Camus

There was also an old poem passed down from my dad's father's mother. My grandfather would often recite it from memory. It has some good advice as well:

> "Don't hunt after trouble,
> But look for success.
> You'll find what you look for,
> Don't look for distress.
>
> If you see but your shadow,
> Remember, I pray,
> The sun is still shining,
> But you're in the way.
>
> Don't grumble; don't bluster.
> Don't dream and don't shirk.
> Don't think of your worries,
> But think of your work.
>
> Your worries will vanish,
> Your work will be done,
> For no man sees his shadow,
> That faces the sun." - Anonymous

Funny how that old country wisdom came to mean more to me, the older I got. At this point though, I had yet to find my "work."

I could certainly relate to Camus' comment, most of all. Hard as it was to go through, and I certainly would not wish to endure that again, nor even wish such a situation on my "worst enemy" (of which I fortunately have none), it seems like this trauma provided the motivation and impetus for us both to grow in ways we probably would not have done otherwise. Thus, all's well that ends well. Fortunately, our story had a long way to go before the end.

Chapter Twelve
Betrayal and Forgiveness

I have to be honest here, as to my own shortcomings. I hate when that happens, but you wouldn't get the full story unless I tell it like it was.

Robb had this supposed "best friend" whom I couldn't stand. They went back many years, certainly from high school days, if not before. I'll just call him "Dick Vogel" (another name changed to "protect the guilty" – certainly, the first name I've assigned him here fit his personality.)

Vogel was a user, in my not so humble opinion. He obviously looked at women as nothing more than sex objects and a feather in his cap. He was a womanizing player and a predator, and those are the facts. For the whole time we'd been dating, I'm sure that Vogel had tried to get Robb to break up with me. I can see as much in one letter Robb wrote me from jail:

Letter from Robb, from Washoe County jail:

"Mary, Well, I'll choose your way over Dick Vogel's any day, because it's better and more like the way I really am. Dick's always been there when I need him for help, and we enjoy the same things. I love you, Mary, but you never once made an attempt to watch me jump, ski, or other things I like to do. I know you had studying to do, and that it isn't very exciting to watch me ski or jump, but that's what I like to do, and other women I've known could ski, or get with some of my interests (male ego) and I became used to it. You are completely different, and I found myself catering to a lot more of your interests than you with mine. Example: babysitting, watching that movie. I didn't

enjoy those things, and I didn't learn anything, so I can see no difference between me doing that and you watching me ski or jump. Dick couldn't either, and therefore tagged you as some chick trying to get over on me, and started his own crusade to save me for my own good. I saw the good and bad in the middle, and stayed there. I've never trusted a female before, but I trust you now, and that's going against what I've experienced with women. I could put my faith in Dick, and know that I would receive the moral support I need, and I'd have a friend when I got out. I'll trust you because I believe in you and your ideas.

"I won't talk about the airplane thing (lawyers), but it was wrong, and I didn't consider any consequences, because I knew I wouldn't fail. What a shock it was!

"Don't give that hardened criminal idea a second thought. You read too many books and statistics, and I don't fit in those facts any more than you do. Trust me on that, okay? I will change a little, but it will be for the better, I assure you.

"I wish I could talk to you for a couple of hours in private. Love, Robb p.s. let's take up some common interest when I get out – some sport or outing."

I so wanted Robb to dump this Vogel fellow as a friend, and be done with it. I guess Vogel and I had a real mutual animosity thing going on.

Robb had been locked up in prison for some time, with us not knowing if he'd ever get out early. A 30-year sentence seems an eternity to someone who is 22 years old. What if it took the whole 30 years; we'd both be 52 by then. Well, that mid-life age sounded like one foot in the grave to us back at that time.

No, I had to go on and live my life, and of course I was worried about the future, and feeling ever so alone and forlorn. By this time, Robb was already serving his 30-year sentence at the federal prison in Lompoc, California.

Predator on women that he was, one night in October 1972, Vogel came by to see me, and his intentions were not of the highest. I could see that right away. The thought flashed through my mind, *"Well….this might be the ONLY way to make Robb see what a creep and user this guy is."* He was somewhat attractive, and I was feeling vulnerable, so I submitted to his advances. It was clear from things he said that he'd been lusting after my supposed charms for some time. I don't flatter myself here; Vogel lusted after anything in a skirt. He had just come over to prey on me, like any of his other female victims, when I was down and lonely and Robb wasn't around to protect me. Why couldn't Robb see what a cad this guy was?

I wrote Robb about it right away, with a *"See, I told you what this jerk is made of"* attitude. Apparently, Vogel wrote him with the same account that I had supplied. Too bad Robb chose to feel hurt about that incident versus using it as the revelation about his so-called friend that I had meant for it to be for him. Sure, that was a naïve attitude on my part, but I was just 22 then, and had some tunnel vision going on. It did hurt him, I shouldn't have done it, and he reminded me plenty in several letters that it was a "_____ up" on my part, to quote him.

From Robb in Lompoc Federal Prison, October 21, 1972:

"Hey, I guess you have all kinds of problems…. Your idea about you and Vogel sounds good, theory-wise, but the best friend takes girlfriend away seems a proven fact throughout history…. I received your letter and his letter today, and they said the same thing, so I guess you don't need my approval or anything. You have to do what you want, I guess. If I had my way I'd freeze you for three years, but I dream a lot. As far as I'm concerned you have always seemed very insecure to me ever since the day I met you. You seemed to handle it well and seemed a lot better off than most people. You seemed a lot more secure than me, but then I really never wanted to be secure. Insecure or not, I try and enjoy life wherever I am. I love you and I don't want to lose you. I can love you and dream of a

brighter day, and stay out of trouble. Without something to hope for and someone to love, it would be twice as hard. I want the best for you and I want you to be happy. So whatever it takes to be happy, do it. Just remember that I need you, because I want you…. Hope you can make it down here to see me next week, and good luck with all your problems. I love you, Robb"

Robb obviously needed to do more processing of this event, and wrote me another letter the next day, October 22, 1972:

"Mary, Well, I thought a lot more about that idea of you and Dick getting together, and here is what I think is good and bad about it. In the future one of us 3 is going to get hurt. When I get out, I would feel very uncomfortable when around both of you (but then again I may learn a lot about life in the meantime and not feel that way, but I doubt it.) …. I think eventually anyway that you'll have to find someone to really love, and who loves you so why delay that. Now on the good side of your idea, I see you using Dick as a sex object and building your ego back up, so that you can go and find a relationship that isn't physical. I know you need someone, and I know Dick needs someone, and you could probably help each other. I've never seen anyone use Dick before, and I don't know if you could or not. You two could fall in love out of a need for each other, and then I would be hurt, and when you both found yourselves again you would be hurt. I really don't know where your head's at, and what you can or can't handle. This is how I feel about the information I have received. If I knew more, I might feel differently. It's not up to me anyway, and probably won't be the biggest problem of my or your life. I do hope you can make it down next weekend, and I hope that whatever you decide to do works out for the best. Only you know where you stand and what you can do…. Stay calm, relaxed, and just live life as it comes. If you have something to hope for, someone to love, and something to do, then you're on the right track. Write soon. Don't bite your fingernails and remember that I love you, Robb"

Reflecting back on this incident after so many years, I cannot help but wonder if there was more to it than my giving in to my own lost and vulnerable feelings. Was there some passive/aggressive anger in me at Robb for doing this stupid crime and wrecking all of our plans for the future? That's possible, but I was surely not feeling that consciously at the time. I was just feeling depressed and abandoned. And as strange as it may sound to everyone – especially to Robb – in some very strange way, Vogel and I were the closest thing to Robb, that each of us had left. He was the best friend, I was the girlfriend, and neither of us really knew if we'd ever see Robb again. After all, Vogel was the one who came looking for me that night, and not the other way around.

Amazingly, Robb was a big enough person to forgive us both for that one time event, and bless him for that. Though he may not know it, his forgiveness, love and understanding reinforced my desire to become a better person. We didn't talk about it much further, as life moved on, at least for me. He didn't have much to do in prison to occupy his time, but read a lot of books. I sent him some good ones, and he pressured me to read J. R. R. Tolkien's *The Hobbit* and then the *Trilogy*. Okay, I resisted for a while, but finally read them, and yes, he was right. They were good.

Robb did mention the Vogel incident in one more letter from Lompoc dated November 6, 1972:

"Well,......on the you and Vogel thing, I don't care if you see him again or not. What's done is done there, and I can't be hurt any more.... Dick Vogel does his own thing. Whether it's for the challenge, intrigue, or whatever. He usually makes it and he's my friend because he's that kind of winner. He's a good person and he never slept in a bed where he wasn't really wanted. He does come right out front with what he wants, and beating around the bush is something he quit doing a long time ago.

Say yes or say no is all he wants to hear. You can't blame a guy for trying.

"Hey, forget those suicidal thoughts. <u>You</u> are my life, Mary. Hey, I really love you. Who'd wash my back, teach me to spell, make me hang up my clothes, save used tea bags, and love me. If things get rough you could always move down here, but do remember that <u>you are mine.</u> Just because you're from the South, doesn't mean you're a loser. I'm not the greatest man in the world, but you're stuck with me. If you can do better, go ahead, but I'll be somewhere if you need me.

"Go ahead and write and tell me all that's happening and all your problems. My head is feeling better and I can handle it all. Don't bring Vogel on a visit though. I still haven't straightened that out yet. Probably won't. Write soon. Love ya forever, Robb"

Robb was also a very good sport concerning my feminist focus. I had taken some honors women's studies courses in college and made it my mission to educate him on the main points. He actually saw the value in much of what I said. The fact that he even read the copies of *Ms. Magazine* that I sent him shows what a trooper he was.

When a man's in prison, I guess he will put up with a lot, to keep the interest and connection to his woman back home. Some of the humor in these letters still gives me a good laugh even as I read them today. He wrote on November 8, 1972, of an ant invasion of his cell, which was funny and well written.

"....My cell was invaded by ants the other day. I don't know where they came from, but it looks like they're here to stay. I've killed off at least a thousand of them, but this war looks like another Vietnam. They started attacking in large numbers, but now they rove around in small guerilla bands. Why me?"

When two people who love each other are separated by time, distance, and circumstance but still able to stay in touch with one another, even sharing laughs over the small things keeps the heart connection alive, like a long distance touch or hug.

Here's an example of his humor from a letter dated November 12, 1972, from Lompoc, as he continues with the ant saga. In prison, they called their jail cell their "house."

"Well…I have decided that violence is the only way out, and I started solving all the world problems by killing every ant in my house yesterday. I know it's a small start, and that you can't solve all your problems with violence, but I only saw one ant today and he won't be back to tell anybody.

"I hate it here sometimes. I'm running out of little things to say, but since you seem to be an aide, complaint and assistance person, I want to say right now that I hope your cat has 9 kittens and they tear up your house, and you learn that cats are <u>users.</u>

"I think you're beautiful and wonderful and smart. Love, Robb"

For decades, I've kept this notebook of all the letters Robb wrote me from Washoe County jail in Reno and then during his time at Lompoc Federal Penitentiary in Lompoc, California. I had not even opened it since the last letter went into it, back on July 15, 1975.

I guess I must have sensed that one day I may want to write a book about this amazing chapter of our lives, and that time has finally come.

Many times while reading these letters in the present day, I laughed out loud at Robb's sense of humor, and his dry wit, getting back at me for being so hard on him about his spelling and grammar.

Other letters were very poignant and touching. I could feel how much he missed me, and it just made me miss him more, too. In one of my favorite letters from him, he spoke about how he loves my mind.

How can a woman not love a man who tells her he "loves her mind" – sure, that could be just a "line" but in this case, I knew it was true. I shared everything with him from my anthropological focus, my desire to go to Africa and study the cultures there, to my feminist Women's Liberation concepts and now…my entire spiritual awakening, knowledge and experiences.

He wanted to learn TM and that program had been available in the Lompoc prison in the past, and they were hoping to get it going again, but always some funding or political issues kept that from happening. It's just not the same at all, trying to read about meditation from a book. It really does take personal instruction from a qualified TM teacher, to be effective.

When Robb first arrived at Lompoc penitentiary, he *wrote* "Well, this place is a real fun house compared to the county jail" (letter from Lompoc September 5, 1972). There were certainly some dicey times there though. He wrote me in one letter dated February 27, 1973:

"Mary, I really want to see you again soon. You stayed away too long last time. I love your long hair and I hate seeing you leave. I love you.

"Almost had a riot today between the blacks and Mexicans. It was very real, and vibrations are everywhere. Hope things stay calm."

I certainly worried about him; but I felt so powerless to help him.

He was doing as much as he could to improve his skills, considering his environment. He became a welder, and actually made some rather artistic statues and other items. Then he was working in the prison lab and decided to become a certified lab technician. He wanted to transfer to the federal prison in Springfield, Missouri for a while, where they offered that program. It took some time, but he finally got there. Once he arrived, he saw that the environment was much worse than at Lompoc.

His parents traveled that distance to see him in Missouri, but I just couldn't make it there. Speaking of Robb's family, they suffered another tragic loss a mere one year after Robb skyjacked the plane and went to prison. Their younger son Don had recently become a born-again Christian or in the parlance of our day, a "Jesus freak." I didn't know him very well but he sure seemed like a sweet, quiet kid.

It was June 22, 1973, and I had a chance to go up to the beach at Lake Tahoe for the day, with a couple of my Harrah's Hotel Casino fellow employees. We went to Sand Harbor. It was such a strange day. We had to wrap up in jackets it was so cold. I watched the waves. They looked black, ominous, and foreboding. I had never seen the waters of Tahoe in such a condition. The vibes were pretty bad. Little did I know then, but not far away Robb's brother Don was on a boating outing with some of his friends. One fellow was floundering in those choppy waters and about to drown, so Don jumped in to save him. The other kid made it to shore but Don did not. He was only 21 at the time that he lost his life, trying to help save his friend's life. I felt so sorry for their parents and sister as well as Robb's grandmother and Uncle Ivan. They had already gone through enough loss to last a lifetime.

Robb got to come home for just the day of the funeral, accompanied by two deputies. He looked so good in his suit. I was allowed to sit with him in church, but there were so many of his relatives wanting to see him. The pictures I have of that day show that though I was trying to smile, I just couldn't. It was all I could do to hold the tears back. In his next letter to me, he wrote about missing his little brother and feeling sorry that we didn't have much time to talk, but there were so many people there. I could tell he was simply overwhelmed by the stimulation from the much different environment than the prison he'd been stuck in for a year already. He mentioned how he wasn't used to so many things happening at once.

When I graduated from college, my big focus was to live with him and start our happy life together as a couple. I didn't have a job for a while, or even a car. Finally, I found a job at Harrah's hotel casino in Reno. I started out as a desk clerk/cashier (yes, a fine way to use my anthropology degree) and later transferred over to their payroll department.

Robb had given me grief about getting an anthropology degree in the first place, feeling that I should have gone for a business degree. But that was so uninteresting to me. I've never felt driven by a desire to make money or have a big, grand career in this lifetime. Apparently, I've had past lives that were focused on that one-pointed pursuit of the Almighty Dollar, so I was not going to make that mistake again. That was not the path my soul had chosen for me in this lifetime.

Finally, I was able to get a used car, and made payments on it until it was paid off. Later I got a job with the Social Security Administration in Reno as a Claims Representative. Oh, yawn. By that time, I was just saving up money to go to TM teacher training in Europe, as what I cared about most was helping people. Teaching TM seemed like the highest calling to me, based on my own experience with this technique.

Plus, David had become a TM teacher earlier and I felt that…just maybe…if I could show him that I was as spiritual as he was, perhaps that cold heart of his would relent and let me in.

Meanwhile, I was still writing to Robb and trying to keep him grounded and in touch with reality outside his prison walls. He responded to one of my letters approximately July 8, 1973. Every time he would try to call me from prison, I was never at home.

"Mary, That was a real good answer to my vague questions. I wanted to talk to you, because I didn't think a letter would do. I've made up my mind to do this sentence to the best of my ability, get out, and stay out. Sometimes the distortions of reality get a little out of hand, and sometimes lead to disastrous plans. I need to hear a voice that rings clearly of the truth and right things to do. You did and do that very well. Thank you. I love you, forever, Robb"

Meanwhile back at home, I was going through my own angst and contemplating what my future might look like. Here is my journal entry from July 6, 1973:

"Why do I feel so strongly? Why do I care for people so deeply? My friends are so important to me. Why do I let these feelings of loneliness overcome me at times; why let time seem so important? Am I only giving in to fears? Cravings to communicate on a deeper level. Time spent in thoughtful conversation with friends is well-spent; it is wasted only on the trivial. There are passions in me not yet stirred. I long to feel that joie de vivre I've tasted on occasion. To open arms in universal embrace and to feel that embrace returned fully. How is it that I seem to learn mostly from suffering... in my loneliness? Does it have to be this way?

"And what of the future – if Robb changes in a way different from my beliefs – must I content myself with the knowledge that I once felt a love that was reciprocated in kind, even though separation cut it off at the bud? 'It's better to have loved and lost then never to have...' bah. I need love. How am I ever to find direction without a teacher?"

It is interesting that later that very month I did find a teacher. I was instructed in the Transcendental Meditation technique on July 28, 1973, at age 23, which changed my life forever, for the better.

Back when I was finally ready to learn to meditate, I wanted David to be my teacher but he, rather wisely, referred me to his TM teacher friends, whom I'll call Jack and Leslie Ramos. Because they had a meditation center in Reno, it would be a much easier four day course for me there than trekking down to Carson City for the four day course with him, and ...because of our personal relationship, he felt this was for the best.

Chapter Thirteen
My Personal Growth Continues

There was a lot to learn once I got on my spiritual path, and I felt a desire to make up for lost time. I read many books based on the work of Edgar Cayce, an American mystic who was able to give readings and help people with long-term health problems, sometimes seeing into their past lives to find the source of current health conditions. His Association for Research and Enlightenment is still active in Virginia Beach, Virginia. One book that I found especially helpful was Ruth Montgomery's *Here and Hereafter*, which I sent a copy of to Robb, while he was in Lompoc. I also read Gina Cerminara's *Many Mansions*, which added some helpful understanding about karma and reincarnation.

As my spiritual studies progressed, the only thing that made sense to me was that we have lived many lifetimes, made mistakes along the way, and have had to come back to right the wrongs in the balance sheet of life, learn our lessons, pay our dues, and progress towards an enlightened state in which mistakes are no longer possible. It's called Cosmic Consciousness and that was what I was aiming for.

One time driving with my cousin and his wife Bonnie in their Volkswagen Beetle, I was in the backseat with David. I remember asking him in so many words, "*What do you want to be when you grow up?*" meaning what career aspirations did he have. He said with a laugh, "*I just want to be.*" He had done maybe a year-and-a-half of studies at Washington University in St. Louis, and then dropped out. He briefly checked out the Haight-Ashbury scene in San Francisco, and got caught stealing a loaf of bread there. Shades of Jean Valjean? That was about as "hippie" as it got for David, and he was soon out of there.

My cousin Jay and his wife Bonnie were expecting a baby at that point. David made a statement that I thought was rather insensitive but possibly true. He said to Bonnie that if she would have been meditating throughout the whole time she was pregnant, she would "have a different soul in that baby's body" – well, gee, we hadn't thought of that. But, what a thing to say to an expectant mother. That's what I mean by a Mr. Know-It-All.

I kept a flame going for David for eight years, from the time I met him when I was 16 and he was 17-and-a-half, until I was 24. I saw him at a TM residence course up at Squaw Valley in 1973. I had gotten close to my meditation teacher and his wife, Jack and Leslie Ramos, and I was helping them organize and sign in the course participants.

We were eating lunch at the same table with our keynote speaker, famed and beloved spiritual teacher, Charlie Lutes. David came walking by with his tray of food and hesitated for a minute as though he would sit with us, but it felt like in seeing me there, he deferred and went to a table at the far end of the room.

Okay, that did it for me. If I could do all this spiritual work, appreciate the same type of knowledge he was so into all of these years, do my meditation faithfully twice a day, and STILL not be good enough for him, Lord, I give up.

Once at the Ramos' house, Leslie and I had been sunbathing out in their yard on a hot summer day. David came by to see Jack and as he walked by, he said something like *"Ooh, la, la, the Riviera."* He had a friendship with Leslie and they could joke around with each other easily. She later told me that she had asked David if he felt anything for me, since she knew from my past life reading that we had been married in an ancient Egyptian lifetime. He grudgingly admitted, *"Maybe a little bit."* Gee, thanks.

I got tired of the "I recognize you at a soul level, but you don't recognize me" game. That was it for me, so we lost touch for many years, especially after I later married Robb.

In reading my journals from that time, I see where I did a lot of writing about David then. There was such a longing to be loved and accepted by this man whom I found so special. There is only so much rejection a person can take.

David appeared in my dreams at times, even for many years after I last saw him in 1974. In these dreams, he was always rejecting me. Some psychic later told me that in these dreams he represented a part of me that was not accepting some other part of me. Wow, heavy, but it sure gave me something to think about.

I also see how many times I wrote in my journal that if I couldn't be with him, then I'd just have to remain alone. What did I condemn myself to? There's nothing like being young and overly idealistic on the Higher Love concept, eh?

Mostly my journals are filled with the pain and sorrow of being alone, for so very many years. There was always a soul yearning to unite with my true Soulmate, or as my spiritual reading expanded, with my Twin Flame, once I learned about that concept.

Twin Flame or bust. Oh, what a dreamer I was to set the bar so high. One of my earliest, simple writings from age 16 when I was still in South Carolina described what I was looking for. This is one of my very first ever journal entries:

> "Success – Money – Love
> If I find what life means to me and am true to myself, I have success.
> If I am truly happy with my friends, and fulfilled and content in my work, I am rich.
> If I ever know a Being with whom I can share knowledge, beauty and the joy of life, I will have love."

In the early '70s, I was pining away for the elusive, cerebral David, and Robb was in prison pining away for his freedom. For

Robb I was a connection to love and life on the outside and I really tried to be there for him. After a while, I got so involved with my spiritual path and he was so immersed in the "prison vibe" that our writing slowed way down. I think we just exchanged birthday cards and Christmas cards for a couple of years.

Robb wrote me on July 6, 1973, that the other skyjacker serving a sentence in Lompoc prison got a three year set off. A "set off" or put off is a little bit like the parole board saying "don't call us; we'll call you." I could tell that this news was a real downer on his spirits. How could it not be? The days of our lives were just passing by, with no end in sight to our separation.

It was May 1975, when we learned the parole board had turned down his request and put him off for three more years before he could come back and ask them again to be released. Here's my journal entry of May 29, 1975:

> "*I wish you peace as the time unfolds.*
> *It's a three-year set off, I've been told,*
> *Before you can again face the parole board.*
> *If only I could, you know, I would fan the depths of your soul*
> *With a soothing breeze to span from here to eternity.*
> *Just take it easy, don't get hot,*
> *Even on the outside, this world's not the greatest spot,*
> *To Be.*
> *But this will change.*
> *We'll meet again one day, you'll see,*
> *But you won't be you and I won't be me,*
> *For in a brand new life we'll have a different identity.*
> *If I could but share with you*
> *What I've learned in three long years*
> *Since our time was through,*
> *It would ease your fears*
> *But then one day you'll find it for yourself.*"

Chapter Fourteen
Off to Europe to Become a TM Teacher: A Key to Robb's Freedom

By October 1975, I had saved up the funds to quit my job with the Social Security Administration, put my meager college student type belongings in storage at some friends' house and off I went to Vittel, France and then Interlaken, Switzerland for six glorious months of TM teacher training. This was a big international course and I met interesting spiritual seekers from all over the world. This included someone who was to become my Best Friend Forever, Laurie Schweickert, who I sat next to on the plane from Los Angeles to Zurich.

This program included six months of extra daily meditations, learning all the scientific knowledge and many modern studies behind this profound ancient technique, as well as learning the actual steps of instructing others in the practice.

I have many happy and cherished memories of this time and a deep gratitude for all the precious knowledge I received. It was also an opportunity to melt away years and lifetimes of stress.

For the first six months of my meditation practice back in Reno, in every twenty-minute session the tears would just stream down my face like a river of sadness. My system was releasing a lot of the stress, shock, and pain that I went through right after Robb committed his crime.

While I was on the course in Europe, I was so touched by how this meditation technique can help others that I naturally thought of Robb. *"He simply must get to experience this meditation,"* I thought, so I wrote him about it, once again.

By this time, Robb had been moved back to the Lompoc prison after lab technician training at the prison in Missouri; it was a much better environment there in Lompoc.

One of the distinctions Robb had accomplished was to be the only white guy on the basketball team there, made up of black guys. His ability to get along with all types of people had always impressed me.

I couldn't help but wonder what kind of life we may have had together, had he never skyjacked that damn plane. Well, now I was on a mission to get him initiated into Transcendental Meditation and I knew just the person to do it – me.

Robb had been able to spend time in some type of "honor camp" at the prison due to his good behavior, and general likability, I think. He had gotten an Associate's degree in Accounting by then, so by some miracle they were letting him come home on a four-day pass. That was just enough time for him to experience the four-day TM instruction.

I saw him when he got to Reno and felt that heavy "prison vibe" on him. The first thing he wanted to know was, *"Are we going to have sex?"* and my answer was no. That wasn't what this was all about; if he had to get those needs served, he could make a trip out to Joe Conforte's Mustang Ranch for that. I imagine he did, but I never asked. It was time for him to get on the spiritual jet track to enlightenment. On December 21, 1977, I taught Robb to meditate.

He had already received "put offs" the two times he'd gone before the parole board earlier, which left him in limbo, having no clue as to when he might ever get out on parole. Once he started meditating, I emphasized the need for being regular with the twice-daily practice, and said to him, *"If you will keep it up, regularly twice a day, your whole life will change in six months."*

That was something we often said to new initiates. This time it was more predictive than even I could know. Six months later, he went before the parole board once more and this time THEY LET HIM GO FREE! What a blessed miracle. It was a time of rejoicing.

He'd been in there for six years by the time he was released. Wow, we both could hardly believe it, and I'm sure his parents were overjoyed. We were so eager to finally begin our life together. It seemed amazing that we would at last have our chance at happiness.

In one letter from Robb from Lompoc prison dated May 5, 1973, he was discussing a visit by a couple we'd both known in high school. They were married now but it was a very out-of-balance marriage, which Robb could see, as it was "all about" the guy. Robb mentions here that the wife was the one with the education but she was the one cleaning the house, etc. (That marriage did not last, by the way.) Robb *states, "I liked the visit very much, but they reminded me of how much I love you and how different their relationship is from ours. Ours is ahead of our time, but I screwed it up anyway. Sorry. I do care, and I was trying. Next time. Love, Robb"*

Well, that was a compliment and I'm glad he saw that our relationship was ahead of its time. He wasn't too happy about the fact that when he got out of prison, I was not in town. I was eager to see him, too, but I was off on a long-planned course at Cobb Mountain, California, to get some advanced meditation training. I had already paid for it and I wasn't about to miss it. Besides, I had this strong feeling that his family would greatly appreciate having a few weeks alone with Robb, without me around. I was right about that.

There were times Robb seemed to get the idea in his head that he could be my "boss" and tell me what to do, where to move, and so on. Now he really wanted me to change my plans and be there right when he got home. I understood that desire, but after my waiting for him for six years, I figured he could wait a month for me. That being-ordered-around stuff did not fit my concept of equality as life partners.

When he arrived home in Reno, his family took him to the Midwest to visit his grandmother. I later learned that he got together there with some old girlfriend or some woman he knew from school. Well, it had been six years since he'd had sex, so though I didn't like it, I also understood. He was holding a bit of a grudge against me for not being there in Reno the second he got out anyway. Okay, fine; now we were "even" for the Vogel incident.

For years Robb's dad and I had had a not-so-subtle tug of war as to who was going to "save Robb's soul" in our own stubborn ways. His dad's approach was a Baptist kind of fire and brimstone, and during Robb's time in prison, I know he had enough Bible pages stuffed down his throat to gag a mule.

I'm sure it was uncomfortable for Robb to be in the middle of this tug of war. He addressed it in a letter to me, from Lompoc prison, dated October 5, 1973:

"....My dad has had his ideas since before you were born. He is very set in his ways, and is very brilliant as a chemist. He makes good money, takes care of business, and on and on and on. I see no need for there to be any conflict between you two. You both think you have the right path for me to travel. You both think I'll listen too much to the other. I think that everything is an opinion, and that mine is as good as anybody else's. I love you both, and shine on a lot of both sides. Two people trying to help a person is not all that easy.... Love ya always, forever and ever, Robb"

Of course, MY way was the more enlightened path of inner transformation through practicing daily meditation. Though I'm sure that his parents looked at us living together as "living in sin," that is what we did, the minute I got home from my Cobb Mountain course. We were immediately planning how Robb could get these advanced techniques, which I had acquired, too, as we were planning our wedding.

Oh yes, after anxiously waiting for him through all his time in Vietnam and then six years in prison, we were finally able to get married! His dad actually said, *"You guys don't have to get married on my account,"* meaning please don't do it based on his religious views. That is actually how much he didn't want his son to marry me! Robb's mom was kind and sweet, but his dad....we just didn't see eye to eye.

Well, too bad, you lose, Pop, and so does Vogel with his meddling interference, as this was now going to finally be OUR TIME.

Robb had written something about wanting to "save" me once he got out, and I wasn't sure what he meant. I thought my meditating friends of the time were all good people, but Robb had a type of savvy insight into human nature, that let him know when certain folks were not what they seemed. To explain all that occurred in that category would take another whole book. When he was out and we were back together, he was very helpful in "saving" me from certain people who proved they did not deserve that cherished title of "friend." I have always taken my friendships as such a gift and blessing, and put my energy into being as good a friend as I can possibly be. Thus, I don't let go of friendships lightly, and many of mine have been life-long. It was another spiritual wake-up call to find out that some who "talked the talk" could not in fact "walk the walk" of having the true spiritual integrity that was essential for me in interactions with others. I had to let go of some whom I had really trusted, and that was hard.

Now, finally we had our chance to be together again. We got married after living together for just a couple of months. Robb was rather jealous of the time it took for me to do my advanced meditation program, so fortunately we got him on a similar course for that training fairly soon, and that made a big difference, to be able to do our daily spiritual practice together.

Together we ran the Reno TM Center, as I took turns being Center Chairman with another teacher couple who lived there, and made that a big success. There were plenty of good friends of mine he met and enjoyed friendships with, too. He fit right in with everyone and seemed to be enjoying our social life with the other meditators. We had a regular group meditation program going on, which produced a nice effect in our town at the time. I still have the newspaper articles; some entitled "Police Unsure

Reason for Reduction of Crime in Reno." They may have been unsure, but we had the sociological studies providing evidence that where there is a large number of people meditating together, crime rate goes down.

Someone asked me if I wasn't afraid that Robb might have another lapse of judgment and commit yet another crime. Well, no, I didn't think that. However, all that had happened to us did bring out the motherly, protective nature in me, which can be not such a good thing in a marriage. I've learned over the years, that men enjoy the tender, nurturing aspects of "mother energy" but not the nagging, critical, or controlling aspects of same!

Chapter Fifteen

Another Surprise:
Seeing the Karmic Scales Get Balanced

G oing back to Vogel for a minute; yeah, just when you thought we were done with that character. He was one friend who was not there to welcome Robb home when he got out of prison. The Universe has some amazing ways of dealing out "instant karma" or in some cases, not so instant. I had a front-row seat to that Life Lesson.

He had gone on to marry a woman whom I will call Jane. She had a child from a previous relationship. One day the three of them were attending a football game at the UNR stadium. A freak wind picked up some board that was lying around, hit the young child, and killed him. Very tragic. Too bad some of Vogel's karma had to rub off on her and her child.

One of the big surprises I got on one of my visits to Robb down in Lompoc was his admission to me (after I'd slept with Vogel the one time) that his "best friend" had actually been the one to drop him off at the Reno airport for the skyjacking mission that day. What the HELL? I was incredulous. I asked *"Do you mean he was planning to split the loot with you and everything, while taking none of the risks*?!!" From what I can recall of Robb's comments, that seemed to be the case. What a real son-of-a-bitch, ratfink jerk. He should have tried to talk Robb out of this act, instead of abetting him.

Wow, if I had hated the dude before, now he would have felt the wrath of God had I seen him, that's for sure. He had been going on, living his life free as a bird, pursuing all his dreams, while Robb was stuck in jail. Of course, I couldn't go back and tell the lawyers or anyone because that would not have reflected well on Robb, this "protection" of his so-called best buddy, and our goal was for him to get out on parole as soon as possible. I kept it to myself all these years, until right now. That creep Vogel even had the nerve to sit with me and Robb's parents in court in August 1972, the day that the judge sentenced him, and squeeze my hand when we heard the decision, "30 years." I didn't know of his actions abetting Robb's crime at that moment, or he would have gotten his own time in the slammer in which to reflect on his very bad behavior.

Back at the time when the skyjacking occurred, I guess one of the reasons the details didn't matter so much to me, was because I was in a state of disbelief that this thing could have even happened. It's only recently that the thought came to me *"Oh, and I wonder WHO followed Robb out to Washoe Valley that day so he could leave his car parked there? Someone had to be picking him up and taking him back home, or was he driven straight to the airport from there?"* There's also the question of just where did he get that gun, anyway?

Now it struck me that perhaps this was one reason Vogel came over to see me that night in October 1972. He may have been worried that Robb had told me about his involvement in the crime, and when he saw that I knew nothing about that, decided to take advantage of me while he was there anyway. Why miss an opportunity to "use" yet another woman? Even if it was his best friend's woman. What karma he created for himself with all of these bad actions!

God has a sense of ultimate payback, and His timing is always the best in any case. Vogel's big dream was to become a commercial airline pilot. He'd been flying as a "bush pilot" for fire jumpers for some years. By this time, he had divorced Jane and was living up in Alaska, with some native girlfriend there, I believe.

Dave Brown had been another of Robb's skydiving team buddies over the years (and he would later become the best man at our wedding). I'd gotten Dave into TM once I got into it, and he got his sister and brother into it as well. Dave was actually a REAL friend to Robb and never tried anything inappropriate with me all those years Robb was in prison.

Anyway, one time Vogel came down to Seattle from Alaska for the weekend and was calling Dave Brown and all his other old Reno friends to tell them his good news. He had been finally accepted as a pilot for a big airline company. Ironically, I think it was United Airlines.

On his trip back to Alaska, as he flew himself there on a small plane, he had a meeting with a different type of destiny. He didn't make it. They say he flew himself right into a mountainside in foggy conditions.

It's not that I haven't long ago forgiven the man, as I am a Christian and that is what we are called to do. It's just that I always thought he was trouble and his character was more than questionable. From the first time I met Robb, I sensed that Vogel was a bad influence, and I resented him for that.

Robb and I went to Reno High School together; I didn't know him then, but I'd seen him around school. The big thing for us teenagers to do in those days was to "drag main" on weekend nights. We had great fun driving back and forth, up and down the main street of the town, right in front of the many casinos and under the arch that said "Reno – Biggest Little City in the World." The red lights would give us time to stop our cars and chat with whoever was going the other direction. There would often be invitations to a "party" or whatnot. More like invitations to a make-out session, drinking, or trouble in general.

That's how Robb and I actually met. He and Vogel were in one car and my friend Bonnie and I in another. We went back to Vogel's place, and poor Bonnie ended up with Vogel for the evening. Nothing happened other than making out, but Robb and I started dating from that time. That was in April 1969. I was in my freshman year at UNR at that time.

Later, when we had a breakup at one point prior to Robb's Vietnam service, I felt sure Vogel's negative influence was part of the problem and cause of that. One of Robb's letters from prison addresses why he didn't get back together with me until shortly before he left for Vietnam. I included the letter earlier on, about how his pride wouldn't let him reach out to me then. Well, I am very sure that part of his "pride" issue was Vogel's desire for him to NOT get back together with me. In the end, the Universe delivered the cosmic justice that this situation apparently called for, and it was certainly not anything I would have ever wished on the man. His number was just up.

Chapter Sixteen
Our Married Life Begins

F ast forward to the future and we were now getting married. We even sent a wedding invitation to H. R. Haldeman, his old bridge-playing buddy from the Lompoc days. I think Robb wanted to show him that he was back into living a happy, normal life.

We got married in Reno, Nevada on October 7, 1978. Robb's parents arranged for us to have the wedding at their Baptist church. I was a bit leery of their minister especially during the ceremony itself. Robb and I had met with him some time beforehand to go over details. I had these lovely passages from a book called *Love and God*, which I wanted him to read, and he agreed to that. This was to be our personal touch in the rituals. Instead, when it came time to read those words, he was up there reading something from 1st Corinthians in the Bible. I wanted to reach up to where he was standing looking so smug before us, and strangle him with my lacy-sleeved wedding-dress hands! What a lying hypocrite. I have no doubt that Robb's dad put him up to that.

Thus, our married life began. We spent the first night of our honeymoon in Mt. Shasta. Robb's grandmother had given him her old 1956 Chevy. It was a gray and aqua two-tone car and had a nice bench seat so that I could sit right beside Robb. That was before we had mandatory seatbelt laws.

Robb made the mistake of having me be the navigator on this trip. Oops. Since that time, I have learned to read road maps very well, but back then, not so much. We headed up the coast, with our goal being the Windemere Motel at Banyon-by-the-Bay, Oregon. Robb wanted to go deep-sea fishing on our honeymoon. The thought didn't thrill me. He could get up at the crack of dawn if he wanted to.

Looking at the map along the way, with him wanting to get there as quickly as possible, I saw a road that appeared as a little dashed line on the map. It certainly LOOKED like a short cut. Ahem. Well, I tried.

It's a good thing that it was a Sunday. This turned out to be a one lane, logging-truck dirt road. We felt lost in the wilderness going over hill and dale. I think we saw one other vehicle and those folks told us where we had wandered, so far off into the boonies from the main road.

"It's another fine mess you've gotten us into, Ollie." Would I ever live it down? We finally made it to our destination.

Robb seemed more into the local activities than enjoying a honeymoon with me. I certainly did not feel like I was his primary focus on this trip. He was trying to cram a lot of outdoorsy and sports events into his life now to make up for his six years in prison. A honeymoon did not seem to me like the appropriate place for that, but I went along with what he wanted to do. I knew he was starved for all sorts of activities he couldn't do in jail, so we went crabbing and walking on the beach. One morning he got up at 4:00 or 5:00 a. m. to head out way too early for the deep-sea fishing adventure. He'd booked time on a commercial fishing boat that took tourists out for those expeditions. Let me sleep, was my mantra. Mother Nature had the last laugh when the boat had to head back to shore almost immediately, due to the winds and waves. So who got up early for nothing? I could not help but laugh to myself about that. My thought was, *"This is what you get for going fishing on our honeymoon, Robb."* In some of his letters home from prison, he had apologized for not being very romantic. To me, a honeymoon is the one place a woman should expect to be treated in a thoughtful, romantic manner. If we women don't get to be the center of our man's attention on a honeymoon, when will that ever happen?

Robb bought a king-size water bed…we are both water sign Ascendants so this should be a nice choice. It was warm, but I never found it that comfortable, though it stayed with us through our entire married life. It was just another one of those '70s innovations that was worth a try.

Thanks to the GI bill and some help from his parents, Robb went back to UNR to finish his education with a Bachelor's degree in Accounting. I was also working full time to support us. He was certainly motivated and ambitious. Our biggest worry was that the local CPA Board may not let him stand for the exam to get his CPA credential after all his accounting studies and efforts to get his degree in that subject, due to his crime and subsequent record. There was a family friend of his parents on that Board. We asked him to check into this possibility for us, before putting in all this time, energy, and money into this educational direction. He could not give us a straight up "yes" on the issue but indicated it looked favorable. It did work out.

I was proud of how Robb had made the most of the time in prison, learning all that he could while he was in there, and then getting his Accounting degree once he was out, finishing up the final two years of his studies for that. In our remaining years in Reno, he became a CPA and was able to get several good jobs. Even one casino hired him. How amazing. He was always honest about his past with potential employers. Here he once had the casinos deliver $200,000 of their money to him to ransom an airplane and its crew, and now he got paid to count money in a casino financial department. The wonders and the ironies of life just never cease.

It did seem to me that many people were just waiting to see if Robb would break any more laws or make any more stupid and serious mistakes, now that he was out of prison. I knew he was going to be okay, thanks to daily meditations that we were enjoying together, but others wanted to see a track record to prove it.

When he first got home, there was still that "layer of prison vibes" on him, but it felt like our daily meditations plus our love for one another was able to wash that off of him. Then he did get to the advanced meditation course, and got those same advanced techniques that I had gotten previously.

I, for one, believe in rehabilitation as I've seen it work. Anyone who would have met Robb once he was free and we were married, could never believe he had done any time in jail, much less six years in the Big House.

He was back to being his fun, sunny self, and he seemed happy. We enjoyed playing a card game, Uno, with a couple of nurse friends, Pete and Joan, who would occasionally visit us and stay at the meditation center in Reno while they did their three-days-a-week work stint at Washoe Medical Center. Those were some happy times, filled with a lot of laughter and good-natured ribbing. By then we were living in the upstairs part of the Reno TM Center at 2040 Idlewild Drive. There were other TM teachers, Jane and David Lewis, who lived downstairs, and various meditators took turns renting the back apartment. It was the perfect setup to host many seasonal celebrations and fun potluck dinners, group meditations, and advanced lectures.

One time, I decided to host a breakfast for all the meditators who we felt were close friends. We set up some big tables and I was busy making omelets-to-order and Robb helped with making the toast and tea. It was a feeling of "spiritual family" and a very warm atmosphere in our TM Center, which was our home for several years. Life with Robb certainly taught me to laugh at myself more. I wasn't going to get my way all the time, but then neither was he. In fact, looking back, I feel he was flexible in terms of going along with most of the important things that concerned me. Bless him for that.

Sometimes meditators from foreign countries would visit our Center. This included Toshio Sanyo from Japan. Toshio could not speak much English, though he could write it a little bit. Robb was wearing one of the matching shirts I'd gotten for us both, which had a heart with wings. Toshio pointed to that shirt and showed he liked it. Robb whipped it off and gave it to him as a gift. Yes, that is the Robb I knew and he was back, giving someone the literal shirt off his back. Interestingly, years later I ran into both Toshio and a German TM Teacher who had visited our Center, Lothar Lontke, as they were both on my first International Vedic Astrology Teacher Training Course that I took on the island of Kauai, Hawaii. Small world, for sure.

We were now 28 years old, which did not feel too old at the time. I had known for a long time that I didn't want to have children in this particular lifetime and Robb seemed fine with that.

There were many happy times, including nice vacations to Tahiti and later Hawaii. Bora Bora in Tahiti remains the most beautiful place I've seen. We really had to scrimp and save for that vacation. This was a place that Robb had long dreamed of visiting. Since we weren't drinkers, we purposely didn't buy into the "food and beverage" part of the package, which our travel agent offered us. He really should have warned us. When we got there, we saw that prices of individual meals were off-the-charts expensive. On Bora Bora we stayed in an individual thatched-roof style little bungalow. The hotel had bicycles we could borrow, but gee, those tires were flat. There we were, riding flat-tire bikes into town to find some shop that sold canned tuna fish and French bread, to bring back to our room. I think we paid for just one or two of the hotel restaurant hot meals the entire week we were there. From my point of view, it was like some early version of the television show, "Survivor." We both discovered how very unromantic I could feel when I am starving.

We also spent time on Tahiti itself and the island of Moorea. The first morning we arrived in the country on a red-eye flight, I was trying to sleep and recover from jet lag, but Robb had other plans. He set an alarm and got us up at some ungodly hour. Like a good trooper, I got on the local islander open-air truck with him to take the drive to the Paul Gauguin museum on the island. No wonder the locals heading for work were looking at us funny. We had gotten there about two hours before the museum even opened. Someone did not have his watch set to the proper local time, it turned out. Patience was a virtue that I had yet to learn at that time. Life with Robb gave me plenty of opportunities to practice same.

A couple of years later, we finally got to Hawaii. We were on the island of Maui, staying at a condo there. Robb must have had some premonition. Ahead of time, he got my aunt to sew a pocket on his swim trunks, with a Velcro closing. He felt that was the safest way to pocket our rental car and condo keys, while we went into the water. Our last day there, we went over to the Sheraton Hotel to enjoy snorkeling and feed the fish there by hand. We had some bread in a plastic baggie so that it wouldn't all melt away at once. It was fun having the fish feed out of our hands. When we got back to shore, thinking we still had plenty of time to get back to our condo, shower and finish packing, Robb realized – uh, oh! He had put the keys into his regular pocket and not the Velcro pocket. They were now long gone.

He spent some time snorkeling out where we'd been in the water looking for them, but he didn't find them. We had to call the rental car place on the far side of the island and just sit there waiting until they came with a new set of keys. Then we had to rush back to the condo and get the manager to let us back into our room. There was very little time left to shower, dry my hair, pack our suitcases, and get to the airport. If only I could have been born with the patience of a saint, but that was not the case. It was a good thing that *"God wasn't finished with me yet"* as I still had plenty of spiritual growing up to do at that point. This turned into a case of *"If mama ain't happy, ain't nobody happy."*

We also went down to Ft. Bragg, California, so he could go abalone diving. He got some nice specimens to make belt buckles of the shells, with his welding equipment. I still have one of those buckles.

Mostly, we enjoyed attending numerous meditation residence courses. I even got him to Cobb Mountain, California on some of these courses and there are some nice pictures from our happy times back then. It felt so wonderful hanging out with others who were on the same spiritual path and had the same interest in personal growth.

Finally, it was clear that things were not really working out so well for us as a couple. I was still very devoted to running the Reno meditation center. He would have liked more time for "normal" things like his many sports events, and to buy our own home. At the time, I only wanted to live in the Center and organize the activities there to keep it the happening place that it was. I taught people to meditate there and held weekly advanced lectures.

I had a cat named Sampson before we got married. Robb took to him pretty well and they bonded. We also had a backyard garden, and did some bike rides through the neighborhood. This was just a few blocks over from his parents' home, in a nice residential neighborhood. To me it was a happy blend of regular married life with a spiritual focus.

Chapter Seventeen
And That's the Way It Goes

S adly, we ended up having different interests. He was the outgoing "jock" type and I had become the meditative spiritual zealot. Since this wonderful technique had saved my life or at least saved my mental health after the skyjacking ordeal, I felt a mission to share this with others and teach as many people to meditate that I could. That's what my focus had become. When he left, he said something to the effect of, *"You aren't wrong; I just don't want to go as fast as you are going."* He was referring to my spiritual goal of reaching Enlightenment. Before things reached that point though, we had some happy times.

However, Robb liked so many outdoor activities that were not my trip. That included fishing and his other preferred sports of golf, skiing, and skydiving. He agreed to give up the latter, as it was rather expensive as hobbies go, anyway. I guess he just wanted me along, watching him play these sports and being some kind of cheerleader at these events, but they were too boring for me. So sorry. I just couldn't get into it, and he couldn't handle how much time and energy I was putting into the meditation activities at the Center.

At one point we tried Dr. John Gray's technique of "Write each other a love letter." John Gray is the author of the *Men Are from Mars/Women Are from Venus* book series. This was certainly a case where my man was from Mars, and I was not.

In this "love letter" technique, we were supposed to write each other all the reasons that it would be good for us to stay together. Then we were to exchange letters and read what the other had written. Mine was long, verbose, talking about our love for one another, and all that we'd gone through together. His was short and just filled with "duty" type sentiments including, *"We should stay together for the sake of the Center."* WHAT? Gee, that letter was so revealing.

I did try some things he wanted to do, like going camping with him on four different occasions. It became painfully clear to us both that my idea of camping was *"to open a window at the Ritz"* to quote a funny comment I heard somewhere. Yes, that fits.

The first time we camped was in a tent on some skydiving group outing out by a lake in the boonies. This was before he even went to Vietnam. There were many others from his skydiving team all around us in their tents. The sleeping bags were directly on the ground. I didn't like it, not one little bit. Where's my hot shower in the morning? Where's the hot and cold running water? *"Use the lake,"* I was told. *"Screw that,"* I thought. *"You don't know who you are talking to, Mr. Outdoorsman."*

The next disastrous camping attempt was out in the desert east of Reno at some place that was supposed to be good for fishing. Robb had all this very OLD camping gear, which he had not bothered to test before taking off in the old Chevy for this expedition. That would include a leaky old air mattress that didn't hold air, and thus our sleeping bags ended up on the cold hard ground that night. It also included a little camp stove that absolutely would not light up. It's a good thing I'd brought along some spaghetti I'd already made, but it was still frozen so we had to chip at it to get to eat anything at all for dinner, that rainy night. When we finally went fishing the next day, guess who was the only one who caught anything? My small fish catch was probably another nail in Robb's deflated ego on that trip, as he caught nothing.

Then there was another tent and sleeping bag trip up north of Reno out in some lovely wooded area, just the two of us. There was a big herd of cows in the distance. I didn't see what was going to protect us from them during the night. Once we were sound asleep, sure enough, I was awakened by the sound of many galloping hooves, headed our way. We got up and looked out and it was just a herd of deer that had run down from the hill above us. Sounded like a stampede to me, and I was all for getting out of there. *"Are we having fun yet?"* Do you really want to know the answer?

The final try was in a pickup with a camper shell, which he borrowed from someone. This time we were in a camping area and a couple of other friends had a similar rig camped nearby us. There was a mattress in the back of our truck (oh joy), but still, what to do at night when one has to climb out and go use the facilities? Trying to climb out of the back of a camper truck in the dark, half-asleep, to find some unfamiliar camping outhouse was not my cup of tea.

When Robb got out of prison, I had my sunny boy back, at least for a while. Many of us have learned that being in love or even being married does not mean "forever," sadly. As the old saying goes, *"A kiss is not a contract"*...yes, well, sometimes a contract is not even a contract, when one party or another decides to break it.

When Robb first wanted out of the marriage, when we were still living in Reno, I asked him if we could try going to counseling. His response was no, because, *"What if we spend all that money, and it doesn't work?"* Wow, so our marriage was not even worth investing in with some new ideas and tools? I could not even lead the horse to water.

We had a separation six and a half years into our marriage. That was a real wake-up call and learning opportunity for me, too. During that time, I read Dr. Leo Buscalia's wonderful book *Living, Learning, and Loving*. One line in his text especially stood out to me: *"No one on Earth is here to live up to YOUR expectations."* Oh, smack myself in the forehead. Guilty as charged. Looking at how my good intentions of helping Robb had now backfired on me, I'm also reminded of some of Bob Dylan's song lyrics, *"I helped her out of a jam, I guess, but I used a little too much force."*

Then I decided to move away to Austin, Texas, as there was a very active, larger TM group there. I drove down by myself, interviewed for a job in the meditating community of Radiance, and got it. So I headed back to get my things, my cat Sampson, and make the move. Robb decided he didn't like being separated from me that much after two or three months, so we got back together. I think mainly it was that he saw I was *"going on a new adventure and he didn't want to miss out on that,"* to paraphrase his comment. He was able to get an accounting job with the same company, so off we went to Austin.

Robb had tried long and hard to quit smoking while he was in prison, and finally made it through that difficult challenge. Giving up drinking was another thing, and there were plenty of drugs to be had in prison, just like in Vietnam. He availed himself of all of the above. I put my foot down when we were married, saying no to all of the above. That worked until we were separated, then he went back to drinking since *"he had not conquered that on his own"* was the story he gave me. He felt, for it to be real, it would have to be his decision.

He also dated a cocktail waitress during our separation period, and trying to be a big person, I gave her a meditation introductory lecture. Later I realized that there was no way I could teach that woman to meditate, as it hurt too much to see her. We put that behind us as we headed off to Austin, in a big U-Haul truck towing the old Chevy. Our cat Sam was riding in the cab of the truck with us and seemed to be enjoying the adventure.

We met many nice new friends in that community and had some good times, other than having to use some chemical bomb in the yard and house to get rid of the fleas that were bedeviling poor Sampson. Everything's bigger in Texas including the fleas. We'd have to keep him pent up in the Chevy so he wouldn't breathe the fumes of those awful chemicals. Gag, choke, such noxious stuff it was.

We lasted for about another six months after the move, and then is was sadly time to part. Robb wanted us to have a do-it-yourself divorce so he got the papers for that. He felt we should part *"before we started hating each other."* Okay, Mr. Positive. How could we ever hate each other after all we went through together? How could this breakup even be happening?

It wasn't my idea, but I was plenty frustrated myself by that time. We seemed to have such different interests. I had to let him ride off into a new life, and he took Sam with him. I couldn't handle flea bombing my rented duplex all the time by myself. The fleas won that battle. My new roommate Barbara would not have appreciated those chemicals in our living space, and she was none too fond of indoor pets anyway. It was enough that we had scorpions and fire ants to deal with around the place.

It was Labor Day weekend, 1985, when Robb and Sam waved goodbye, and then drove away, moving to Fairfield, Iowa, which had another big meditation community. That was a bittersweet experience, saying goodbye to my husband and best friend, and beloved Sammy cat all at the same time.

I stayed in Austin a total of a year-and-a-half myself, and then made a big move to a larger TM community in the Washington, DC area. Off I went, on another new adventure. It was scary and exciting at the same time, as I knew very few people there.

I was going to try to get excited about my own new single life and make the most of the change, too. I did get one nice card from Robb, with a shining golden, glimmering cover on it, after he moved to Fairfield, Iowa. He said:

"Mary, You live life like it should be lived. You seem to be getting your share of support of nature and no one deserves it more than you. I want to wish you all the best and tell you that Sam is doing fine except for the fleas. He wishes you well, too. Love always, Robb and Sam"

Those kind sentiments meant a lot to me then, and they always will. I've saved that card, along with all his letters from prison. One thing I have never been able to understand is how anyone can come to "hate" any person they once truly loved. Shakespeare taught us that *"Love is not love which alters when it alteration finds."* I've always tried to understand how and why a person acts the way they do, including making choices that may feel to my detriment. That includes going all the way back to my father's mean treatment of me and my brothers. I had a glimmer of insight that WWII had badly affected him and his nerves. That understanding increased as I got older and learned about PTSD.

When a relationship ends for me, the feelings I have for a person sort of morph into a back burner type of Agape, brotherly love for them. Of course, I will always care about that person's well-being. Why should I allow my own heart to become hardened or shrivel up by entertaining negative and petty emotions? That's not "how I roll." Sure, having no shields or walls as Robb wrote about long ago, has meant that I've experienced my share of painful hurts and disappointments but I'd rather walk through life with an open heart. At least I have attracted a great wealth of the most spiritual, true friends, from having this point of view and maintaining this higher love heart vibration. I have often joked to my friends that I've earned four "Ph.D.s in sainthood" in this life. Some of those stories can be topics for future books.

Robb and I both loved the music of The Eagles. In one letter from Lompoc, he urged me to buy their Desperado album that had just come out. I certainly thought of him whenever I heard their title song played, and still do. The lyrics, written by Glenn Frey and Don Henley, were just so perfect for our situation. Unfortunately, the Eagles would not grant me permission to use their lyrics in my book, but you can find them singing this great song on YouTube, or google "Desperado" to see the lyrics and think of my and Robb's story.

Looking back now at all these old letters from prison and the love Robb was showing me then, I sure wish that I had not been so hard on him, once we got back together. Perhaps I became the Desperado, after too many years of living alone and having to chart my own spiritual course. I was determined that nothing would pull me off of that path, as life-saving as it had been for me, during the most devastating time in my life. Maybe my "cure" had become another type of "prison," but it was what I needed at the time to keep going, and it had become a way of life for me.

Chapter Eighteen

The Wounded Warriors and the Wounded "Waiters": Robb Grants His First Interview After 41 Years

Well, we didn't get to have "forever," but we had enough quality time to make it all worthwhile. In any case, wherever Robb is today in his journey, I certainly wish him all peace and joy and the best things this life has to offer.

Over a year ago, an article came out about Robb and his skyjacking. It was the very first time he'd allowed an interview, after all these years. Here are some excerpts from writer Bruce A. Smith's article that appeared in the March 28, 2013 issue of *The Mountain News – WA*, "The Hunt for DB Cooper - An Interview with a so-called Cooper - copycat skyjacker Robb Dolin Heady". I'm sharing these excerpts because it's good to hear these statements and answers in Robb's own words.

"On June 2, 1972 – six months after he had returned home from Vietnam – Robb jumped over a three-foot-high fence surrounding the tarmac at the Reno airport and ran towards an emptying United Airlines plane. It was Flight 239 from New York, bound for San Francisco, and it had just landed and unloaded its Reno passengers.

"It was sunset.

"Heady was carrying a small reserve parachute and a 357 Magnum that he had borrowed from a friend. He had a pillow case over his head and slits cut for his eyes. After he put the gun to the head of a stewardess, the crew accepted his

demands. However, they insisted that they switch airplanes, claiming the original plane was low on fuel and had a bad engine.

"'There wasn't a lot of planning,' he told me, referring to the skyjacking, 'but I knew it could be done.'

"Once aboard the second plane, Robb demanded that the aft stairs be 'cracked open,' and after receiving $200,000 in hundred-dollar bills they took off, heading for San Francisco. Robb says that no one knew he was going to jump for his escape, but he thinks the pilots surmised his intentions because of his aft door request.

"According to official accounts he jumped at 12,000 feet.

"Robb had intended to land near a highway on the southeast side of Lake Washoe, just outside of Reno, but the pilot veered 'too far to the right' and Robb was unable to correct his position even though he 'tracked' through the night skies at speeds up to 220 mph in an effort to reach his target. As a result, he landed on the southwest side of the lake in Washoe Valley, at an elevation of about 4,500 feet.

"Hence, Robb could not reach the car he had parked near the highway on the other side of the lake.

"'I under-estimated how fast they could seal off the valley,' Robb told me. As a result, Robb was trapped within the Washoe Valley, even though he didn't know it at the time. Robb estimates that he jumped at about 10 or 11 p.m., and the cops found his car with a US Parachuting Association bumper sticker shortly thereafter.

"Figuring the lone vehicle was the skyjacker's getaway wheels, the police put it under surveillance. County sheriff deputies arrested Robb at 5:20 a.m. when he approached the car and unlocked it.

'What's it like to jump from a 727?' I asked.

'Yeah, I guess a lot of sky divers would want to know that, eh?' he said, laughing. 'My body was whipped around pretty good.'

"At the time of his skyjacking, Robb had over 160 sky dives, but this was both his first jet and first night jump. He also said

116

the reserve chute opened 'really hard,' and he waited until far down in his descent and its heavier air before he deployed his parachute. All through our conversation, Robb impressed me as an articulate and knowledgeable skydiver.

"I asked him if he was afraid.

'After Vietnam, nothing scared me,' he replied.

"....The actual jump sounded fairly tricky as he had no idea how fast the plane was flying, but it could have been at least 300 mph.

'I'm sure the pilot didn't show me any favors,' he said with a laugh. 'It seemed like a normal take-off, and I jumped about 20 miles from the airport, as the crow flies.'

"Robb says he tumbled for about fifteen seconds until he stabilized.

'I held my arch (position),' he said, 'and eventually I corrected.'

"Unlike Cooper, Robb created an aerodynamic profile by putting his ransom money into a fishing vest that had three large pockets. He protected the vests by wearing it under a wind breaker.

'The bills didn't all fit in the vest, so I had to leave some money behind – maybe about twenty-thousand,' Robb said. 'I also put some of the left-over bills in a stewardess' purse.'

"Nevertheless, the police reported that they found $45,000 on the plane two days after the skyjacking, but Robb was uncertain how that happened.

'I thought I had left only about $20,000.

'Did you land with the rest of the money?' I asked.

'Of course.'

'But the police reported that you lost the money on the way down.'

'Yeah, that's what I told the cops when they got me,' he said. 'But I buried it when I landed, and then I told my lawyer about it and we were able to make a deal. He went and got it.'

"Robb was sentenced to a 30-year term, but he was released after six years. He served his time in Lompoc federal prison, located in California.

'It was a typical federal prison – lots of federal crimes – bank robbers, drug cases, that kind of thing,' he told me. 'I fit right in, with all of my problems,' he added, again with a laugh. 'Prison was actually a good thing for me. It helped me – being in a structured environment. I read a lot, and I began to feel better (about his PTSD).'

"....Continuing, I asked Robb why he stole the airplane. The conversation reached a greater depth, one of earnest self-revelation.

'I got really messed up in Vietnam,' he said.

"Robb described how he was drafted unexpectedly.

'I ruptured my spleen playing football in high school,' he said, 'and had it removed. That usually keeps you out of the military because the spleen makes red blood cells and without it you can get really sick, like with malaria, which I got in Vietnam.'

"Robb said that the draft rules changed when the lottery was initiated in 1969, and his medical deferment was no longer accepted. Hence he became 1-A and got drafted.

"...Robb entered the army and was assigned to the infantry. However, an opportunity arose for volunteering into an airborne unit, which Robb accepted as it would keep him out of Vietnam for the additional month he would need for extra training.

"However, his plan for minimal exposure to combat back-fired, though, because his new unit was staffed with several gung-ho officers – some fresh from West Point.

"I had some good officers and some bad ones, but a lot wanted to see action."

"These latter commanders were eager for the kind of fighting that resulted in promotions.

"They pushed it, and it rubbed me the wrong way," Robb acknowledged.

"As a result Robb was marginalized, and when his airborne unit rotated home he was forced to serve as a security grunt in

Da Nang. Further, the army didn't want him and his less-than-robust-love-for-authority stateside, so like many other soldiers returning from Vietnam, they discharged him a few months shy of his two-year hitch. Ironically, he was mustered out from Fort Lewis, smack dab in the middle of Cooper Country.

"In Vietnam, Robb served with the 173rd Airborne Brigade of the II Corps, a paratroop unit that functioned as infantry. He was stationed near Pleiku in the north-central part of the country, and it was a jungle environment ripe with combat.

"... Besides enduring the traumas of war, Robb also suffered greatly from a bout of malaria, which he contracted in his fifth month in Vietnam. Without a spleen he was racked with fevers. However, doctors had to test his blood at the height of a fever cycle to ascertain the exact type of parasite that had infested him, which took additional time.

"By the time he made it to the regional hospital at Qui Nhon (pronounced "Quin yon"), Robb says the doctors told him that he should never have been drafted, and certainly not sent to Vietnam. Nevertheless, he returned to his unit upon recovery.

"Perhaps the enormity of his war experience was encapsulated on the night he was flown to Qui Nhon for treatment – twenty-two men from his unit were also med-evacuated because of wounds received in a rocket attack.

"Despite his illness, Robb served the rest of his tour and left Vietnam in December 1971. The effects of Vietnam still lingered, however, and his return to civilian life was difficult.

"I developed a severe case of PTSD," he told me. "I was feeling awful all the time after I got out of the army."

"Emotionally, Robb spiraled downward to the point where he didn't care if he lived or died. From that state he decided to hijack an airplane.

'Why? I didn't have a...ya know...a big reason,' he said.

"Robb expanded upon his state of mind.

'I had been a normal, middle-class guy, and then two years later I'm hijacking an airplane. How does that happen?' he mused.

"...However, when he returned to civilian life and enrolled in school to become a CPA, Robb found he couldn't study or learn in the same way he did prior to his military service.

'I feel that I was brain damaged,' he told me. 'My IQ was about 145 when I went into the military. I know from when they tested me. Now, it's about 120.'

"Robb is still in treatment for his PTSD, and he also maintains contact with a few of his army buddies.

"A lot of guys have PTSD, but they don't think that they do. It's quiet, and it just becomes a part of you. One of them – he can go off whenever the right combination of things happen. He's a ticking time bomb. Lots of guys are like that."

Well, this interview really hits home with me, on several fronts. It explains many things that the early newspaper reports had gotten wrong on the details of the skyjacking. All those chances he took, jumping with just a reserve parachute, his first night jump, his first jump from a jet airplane, from such a high altitude...it all reminds me of just how lucky he really is to have lived through the whole ordeal. That includes from the onset, when they made him change planes at the Reno airport while they had sharp shooters ready to blow his head off, which I'm sure they would have done, if he hadn't put the blanket over his head and that of the stewardess he made walk closely beside him to the second plane. What timing that my uncle in Reno was listening to those events on his police scanner device right as it was happening so I heard about these details.

I am glad to see that Robb has gotten a clear understanding of this PTSD which plagues so many combat veterans, and that he's taken steps to get treatment for that.

We actually had a rare phone conversation on April 13, 2014. He mentioned then that there were experiences he had in Vietnam, which he hadn't even told ME about. It was the first time that he let me know that he'd become aware of his PTSD in recent years. He poignantly said "It's kind of ruined my life." Wow.

My immediate thought upon hearing his comment was, *"And who else's life do you think it's ruined?"* The women who are left behind, praying for the safe return of their soldiers, writing them, keeping their hearts open to welcome them safely home when and if that prayed-for day arrives, that's who. There were so many of us, grateful to get our young Vietnam veterans back, but not having any idea about the "invisible scars" or "time bombs" they were carrying. They came home with Post Traumatic Stress Disorder, but we didn't have the understanding about this condition as we do today. All of us were wounded; the ones who fought and the ones who were there waiting at home, hoping to pick up our dreams of a happy life together upon their return.

I recently spoke to Robb's interviewer and he asked *me, "In what way do you feel Robb's PTSD has impacted your life?"* That's a good question. I'm no expert on the subject of Post Traumatic Stress Disorder but from what I gather, it can make it hard for a veteran with this condition to "be present" with others who are close to them. Maybe I wasn't as present with him as I should have been, either. In any case, I'll always wonder if we could have made it for the long haul, had not Vietnam, his resultant PTSD (which we were not aware of at the time), the skyjacking and subsequent jail term affected the love we truly felt for each other.

Much has been written about "victim consciousness" and we all know how unattractive that looks and feels to be around. I've also read, *"Either none of us are victims, or all of us are victims."* Yes, every life has its share of challenges. I accept my share of the responsibility for why our marriage failed; I was too impatient, not flexible enough, and had not learned all the spiritual lessons I still needed to learn back then. The thing I DO blame the most for the demise of our marriage is the psychological effect of that war and the lack of counseling for our veterans when they returned home. What that did to Robb had a big impact. Things might have turned out so differently if he had not had to go through the stress of those wartime experiences.

Many people speak of having regrets and wishing they could do things over. I'm sure Robb wishes that, in terms of his crime.

I try not to have regrets. Once I had a grounded understanding of karma and how many times we've been around this wheel of life with each other, it just all made sense. This gave me great peace of mind with the many changes that were to come in the future. At one point, I had another past-life reading with a highly clairvoyant friend in Mt. Shasta, California. That gave me even deeper insights on aspects of our connection. In this session, my own awareness was taken to the Akashic Records and I "saw" for myself a different life with Robb. In that one, actions were taken of a nature that his spirit, out of guilt and/or obligation, wanted or needed to create a scenario in this lifetime in which he'd have to spend some time in prison. It's as though he were "doing time" for the previous transgression as a type of penance. We had been married in that lifetime and had a baby then, but….well, enough about that one.

Let's just say, it became clear to me from "seeing" various lifetimes in which I had been a mother, why I was not about to have a baby with him or anyone else in this lifetime. I may have possibly considered it, had I ended up with David, for several reasons, but that just was not to be. We all had "other fish to fry" in this journey. I know that I've been a parent in many past lives and gave my all to that noble calling, but this lifetime was to be dedicated to spiritual growth. That is another decision that I am at peace with.

As a young woman, it was hard to deal with some of the spiritual realities that I later became aware of. I still felt the strong need and desire for a partner, but not just anyone. I needed someone who would understand me and be on the same page I was about spiritual matters. It was to be a long journey, trying to find that.

"If I knew then what I know now"…who knows what different turns I may have made on the path of life. We all operate from the best place we can, with the knowledge we have at the time.

"Knowledge has liberating power" to quote one spiritual teacher. Thus it became my mission to acquire as much knowledge as I could in the spiritual endeavors to which I'd felt led.

The chapters of our lives, they come and go. The main thing we have control over is our reaction and attitude to these events, as so much is simply beyond our control. I've found how important it is to stay one-pointed on our spiritual goals to avoid being mired in disappointments that the many changes in life can bring. Our very wise spiritual teacher Charlie Lutes used to say, *"Keep your eye on the doughnut, and not the hole,"* i.e. stay focused on the things that truly matter.

I am grateful for all I learned in those days and especially for the advanced lectures where I heard Charlie Lutes talk in Reno or several times at retreats in Utah. He was a man's man. Strong, wise, humble from all he'd learned on his own spiritual path, and a successful businessman who looked great in the suits he wore. His stories were laced with such delicious humor. He was also devoted to his wife. Devotion is always a quality that impresses me, when I see it in action. In one of his talks explaining karma, he had such a wise saying that sticks with me to this day, *"Nothing is ever given to you greater than your ability to handle."* There were so many times that I'd have to remind myself of that, in the coming years.

One time at a talk in Utah, I remember that questions came up on the issue of marriage. One smart-ass decided to ask, *"Charlie, couldn't you just marry ANYBODY?"* I loved his answer and we all roared with laughter when he delivered it so well (Charlie didn't tolerate smart-asses so easily and he certainly knew how to spot one) *"No, you couldn't marry just anybody; ANYBODY wouldn't have you!"* Ha, ha. That still cracks me up.

Maybe I am just "easily amused." In modern times, I have a dear friend named Nancy. When we email, half the time I make her laugh so hard she nearly "pees her pants," as she puts it. She thinks my life is so funny that they should make a soap opera out of it. She says the best part is that I don't even KNOW that I'm being funny. Well, anything for a laugh, Nance. It's the next best thing to a hug, I guess. It seems to me that a good sense of humor is essential for anyone on a spiritual path. A good laugh is as liberating to the spirit as listening to our favorite music can be.

Why is this story just coming out of me now, at this time, and why did I save those "letters from prison" all of these decades? I guess it is just time for it. *"Knowledge responds to the need of the time,"* one spiritual teacher said. I'm responding to some impulse of "knowingness" from deep within that it's time for this story to be told. Perhaps it will bring even more healing for me, and for Robb, if he cares to read this book. I hope so.

"All the world's a stage and all the men and women are merely players on it. They have their exits and their entrances, And one man in his time plays many parts," Shakespeare advised us in his play *As You Like It.* Learning what "roles" I have played in countless Earth School lifetimes has certainly made me a more thoughtful, responsive person, I feel. Seeing how the cause and effect of karma with various souls has played out, has been like an "aha" light bulb going on over my head.

Charlie Lutes used to tell us, *"The cops today, were the robbers last time around."* He also pointed out that we are all more evolved today than in any past lifetime, so the past does not matter so much. The value it has had for me though, is to look at the patterns that have come to my attention. If someone was nice and kind to me in a past life, then for sure we have a wonderful heart connection today. If they were awful and even caused my death in a previous life, then there has been tension and not such good interaction in this lifetime. I comfort myself with the thought, *"Well, at least they didn't get to kill me THIS time."* So that's definitely an improvement.

I don't feel so alone any more, having this deep sense of constant connection to Source. I used to be afraid that if I "listened to Guidance" it would lead me to places I didn't want to go and give me even more work to do when I felt I already had enough work to do, thank you very much. Now I'm a better listener and I follow that guidance because it feels right to do so, even when it's also a bit scary to my human self, to take that next step. I've been able to develop skills that I know have been my way to "help the world" and while it has not paid me a big income, it has been fulfilling, to know I have been of service to my fellow man.

Sometimes, when I was still living in Reno, I would get this sense of something pulling me into the future, some intense sensation of wonder, all the "what ifs" and "why nots" playing through my mind. I can recall another evening when I got up and stared out the window into the night sky, thinking about David. It still seems strange to me that I could feel such a spiritual bond with someone and not have that reciprocated. How could God let that be? It was a mystery that I had to make peace with. At times, I would still think about and question the situation. I guessed that maybe it had to do with the energetic reality that until someone really learns to love himself, he is not able to accept love that tries to come to him from anyone else…nor give it to anyone else. How sad is that.

Well, I'm glad I got my "useless" degree in anthropology, and I'm glad that I loved and later married Robb, skyjacker or not. I'm glad I met David and had his influence to get on my spiritual path. I used to kid him that he is the one who got me into anthropology, and then into smoking weed and then, oh no, there shall be no more weed smoking, for we are into meditation now. He became a meditation teacher, and then so did I. In fact, I took far more of the advanced courses after that than he ever did.

May this book be an offering to show that faith and devotion can get us through any dilemma, that true unconditional love is a hard path but a worthy one, that "love conquers all" is not just a saying, and that learning, growing and helping one another is what it's all about. Perhaps this book is part of my answer to the question, *"What are you going to do to help the world?"* Miss Lily Lemon, I sure hope you are proud of me now, from your vantage point in Heaven.

Chapter Nineteen
What Have I Learned?

If I could speak to a younger version of myself, what advice would I give? Stay strong; weather the course; it's going to get better; this too shall pass; all things happen for a reason; learn patience; learn to trust in divine guidance and divine timing; remember to stay positive; remember to laugh at yourself and the foibles of life. You chose to be here at this time on Earth, having these very experiences in order to learn and grow. Fear not, and do not judge yourself for trying and failing. In the end, the only thing you get to take with you is the love in your heart. Be in joy as much as you can, for that is your natural birthright. You'll be a better example to others by the life you lead than the words you speak. Your angels are always with you, and can be called on for help at any time.

Forgiveness – it's always been fairly easy for me to forgive others. I hope this book may be a vehicle to forgive myself for any remaining self-judgments that I may unknowingly hold, at any level. May I forgive myself for any false mental constructs that I may have carried, such as thinking there could have been anything further I could have done to prevent this tragedy. Let me be free of questioning why didn't I see or hear any "signs" of what Robb was about to do, in order to try and stop him before he acted. I give myself the freedom of forgiveness, knowing I wrote to him as long as I could have, I visited him as much as I could, and after he was out of prison, I married him. For better or for worse.

When Robb decided that the patterns in the marriage had gotten too "worse" for him to handle, I forgave him for having to move on. I'm reminded of that Janis Joplin song "Bobby McGee": *"He was looking for a home and I hope he finds it. But I'd trade all my tomorrows for ..."*

No, I won't! I shall not trade one single tomorrow for any man or any lost dream from the long ago past. Every day is a blessing, and a chance to experience the beauty of life. There is also always the hope of new love as long as we stay alert and aware, and committed to our own Highest Good and that of all other beings.

In recent years, I took a course in dream analysis. The teacher said that actually every character in any of our dreams represents some aspect of ourselves, trying to tell us something. In Eastern philosophy, this human life is referred to as the Waking Dream. When we get to the Other Side of this journey we are said to actually "wake up" and then realize that while on Earth, we were really "dreaming" the whole time we were here. In which case, no seeming screw-ups will matter so much after all. Nobody's bigger college degree, higher salary, or initials behind their name will matter one whit more in the game of life. It struck me today that just maybe, if this is a Waking Dream, then everyone I meet is just some type of projection of a part of myself. That is, my/our Higher Self. We all have something to offer, to teach, and to learn together, and benefit from.

A couple of life mottoes have served me well on my life path. One is *"Vasu Dev Kathumbhakum"* which translates as "The world is my family." The other one is, *"The best is yet to come."* I do believe it is.

The Truth shall set you free. It's so funny how that which I do not fear, never turns out to be a problem for me (like talking to the two FBI agents that day). It seems like anything that I allow fear to attach to, whether it's a desire and fear of not having what I want or even just a top-heavy level of energy towards a particular desire, those are the things that have had the hardest time manifesting in my life.

It has not been difficult to write this book, for example. The memories and stories have flowed right from my heart and soul through my fingers and onto the page. It feels like when the time is right for a thing, then it effortlessly flows into our existence, with ease and Grace, and when it's not time for it...forget about it. No amount of wishing is going to make it so.

Not that it is bad or wrong to have a desire. After the divorce, I used to pray to God to take away my intense longing for my soulmate, since for years it just wasn't happening. Well, that prayer seemed to fall on deaf ears for a while, too. Then I got busy with my life work and enjoyed the company of so many wonderful, spiritual friends, it no longer felt like there was a "hole in my life" any more. Besides, there are so many angels hanging out in my home, wherever I live, that I'm going to start charging them rent. Just kidding, angels.

Now, I'm more in that state that David talked about long ago..."I just want to be."

I could write a book alone on the subject of acceptance, making peace with what is, and the resolution to still keep giving and feeling unconditional love, even when one does not get one's deepest wishes to come true. Life is still worth living and such a precious gift from the Creator. I learned to cherish all the wonderful friends I have even more deeply and take comfort in small pleasures since the bigger dreams kept staying out of reach.

One thing that I do blame for destroying my chance at a normal and happy life with either of these men I met when we were so young, is the Vietnam War. I feel that little has been written about the burden and the effects of that war on the women of my generation. How many women, like me, had been writing to their men in service in that far-off country, believing in them and praying for their safe return and a happy future together, only to experience the invisible scars of war having so changed their husbands or boyfriends, upon their return.

We kept the home fires burning and the lighthouses of hope glowing for our men on the battlefields or out at sea. There was often a bitter reward to reap when those men came home. Sometimes the scars were obvious. The ones that didn't show were the worst. Some women became the victims of domestic abuse. Others watched their loved ones sink into depression and then into the pitfalls of addiction to alcohol or drugs. Some had to endure the loss of their loved ones through suicide. These veterans were reaching for any type of "self-medication" to ease the pain of all they saw. They were trained to go into battle, but not to come out of it. Some of them seem to have stayed in it to this day, remaining in that "fight or flight" high stress alert status that soldiers in war have to maintain to stay alive.

Many Vietnam vets live under bridges, homeless in this land of plenty, as that is the only place they feel "safe," strangely enough. Any outreach program needs to reach them "where they live" emotionally and psychologically or help them transcend it through meditation, such as TM's program for "Wounded Warriors" which has had great results in recent years. Many vets credit this meditation with helping them turn away from suicidal thoughts and intentions, as a matter of fact. Still more needs to be done for those who gave so much for their country in its perceived time of need.

Don't even get me started on the "perceived" part. The French failed in Vietnam and so did we. The Russians failed in Afghanistan and it looks like the USA is not doing any better than they did. We've tried to manage some type of peace agreement for decades in the Israel and Palestine conflict and have gotten nowhere. I'm not saying we should not try, but there certainly needs to be a different approach, one that will have some chance of working. It won't include violence on either side if it's to be lasting, of that I feel sure.

The fact that I taught Robb to meditate was to me, one of my biggest gifts to him. Sure, he had to pay the standard little $75 fee that it cost at that time to help keep the Center going, which I never heard the end of, but really, for him TM was a gift. I know that it helped him to readjust to life outside of prison better than any amount of counseling would have done. There is just nothing like taking that daily deep dive within and experiencing the pure bliss, energy, creativity, and release of stress that meditation provides. So in that sense, we both had David to thank, for he is the one who pointed the way (rather firmly) for me to get on this spiritual path, which has worked so well for thousands of people.

My Vedic Astrology birth chart shows that I have a keen sense of fairness. This would often cause me to agonize over whether I had acted in a fair way with others, or whether something had been "my fault" or not. It took many years before I was able to be kinder to myself in terms of that type of analysis. I am confident these days that in every situation, I have tried to consider things from the other person's point of view, and I've been as fair to them as I know how to be.

I guess the thing that hurt the most was not being able to make a greater difference, no matter how much I loved. When I ponder the raw emotion of that statement, it really hits home. A woman feels her greatest gift is the love in her heart. That is why rejection feels so bad, I guess. Love wants to circulate and flow around in a circle from one heart to another. My heart would start that circle of energy flow only to meet a brick wall, in the case of David. It was nearly like a tangible physical pain.

With Robb, he could feel my love, I'm pretty sure, but being stuck in jail there wasn't much either of us could do, other than stay in touch through letters. A few times, he tried to call but I was just not at home. How could I know that he had this PTSD thing that would affect our relationship even when he got home and we got married?

A tale of star-crossed lovers, that is what I felt consigned to, in both instances. My journals reflect some of my feelings of that time. I needed an outlet for my emotions, and all I had was writing in those journals.

If all this time later, Robb wanted out of the marriage after we moved to Austin, then I wasn't going to stand in his way. If you really love a person, you cannot help but want what is in their best interest, according to how I look at life. Sometimes as a couple, two people grow as much as they can together, and then they have to move on to different lessons. Sometimes our souls have made more than one "contract" to live, love, learn, and grow with different partners during this particular journey. A couple of times I've experienced someone "breaking their soul contract" to even get together with me as well, as life has progressed. Now that's rather painful. My reaction has been, "Well, gee whiz, who is going to want me then, if even this <u>soul mate</u> doesn't want me?" when it has been time to meet or reunite with them. Yes, that has not been any fun at all, I must say. I still believe in a Divine Plan for our lives, while honoring and observing more over time how much "free will" we truly have been given, to either screw up our lives or make them Heaven on Earth. The latter is certainly what I wish for all of us.

I have no doubt that getting on my spiritual path and becoming a meditation teacher and later also becoming a Vedic Astrologer was the path that my soul had chosen for me rather than traveling to far-off Africa as a practicing anthropologist. I have no regrets about that.

This was the perfect venue for "helping the world" and I felt I was finally living up to the inspiration that Miss Lemon had placed in my heart all those years ago.

Even with my regular daily spiritual practice for over four decades now, and all the self-improvement courses that I have taken as well, I certainly still do not feel "perfect." I feel that there will always be room for growth and expansion of wisdom, and more opportunities to be of service as well. However, looking back, I am proud and glad of the amount of progress I see. What one focuses on, one becomes. To quote the Founder of our TM program, *"Whatever one puts their attention on, grows in their life."*

I try to remind myself of that bit of wisdom whenever my conscious mind tries to fall back into old fears and worry patterns. Some of those patterns are not easy to overcome when they are embedded in the birth chart one came in with and in the family into which one was born.

Depression runs deeply in our big Irish-Scottish family and I guess many other such clans around the country. There is a saying that, *"This is why the Irish drink."* It's another example of "self-medicating" to hide the melancholy that grows in the branches of the family tree.

That was not typically the case with me, until Robb was stuck in a federal prison with a 30-year jail sentence. There is a photo taken of me at that time, looking so forlorn. My mother was concerned about me and came out to visit my aunt and see me after that. Heaven knows whether she was worried that I would try to do myself in or something, but I am made of stronger stuff than that. It was good to see Mom and I appreciated her making the effort to travel all the way to Reno to see me. My dad never came out, not even later to give me away at my marriage to Robb. He was afraid of flying, and seemed afraid of going too far from home. When we were growing up, I'm sure it was his own safety and security fears, brought on by his experiences in World War II, that brought out the worst in him and caused him to be so harsh with us three kids at times.

My dad has been gone for many years now. Once our mother also passed on a few years ago, I took on the project of typing up my dad's letters home from Europe and Northern Africa, where he was stationed in World War II. His mother had saved every letter, including some that he sent his siblings and others. Amazingly, I could read his handwriting. What impressed me was the brave and cheerful front he was putting up in nearly all of those letters he wrote, as homesick as he was. He served for four-and-a-half years in that war, in the 175th Corps of Engineers, U.S. Army. There are forty-two letters that I found and transcribed. It was only the very last letter, written in May 1945, in which he showed how much the stress and frustration had built up. He had lost faith in believing anything the higher-ups were saying about his group getting to go home, for one thing. As he succinctly put it *"I would consider myself lucky to get to see you all again."*

Taking on this letter-transcription project, I was trying to gain some insight about how my dad was as a young man, and how the influences from the war he had to fight in, shaped him into the person he became upon his return home. It was another case of PTSD, from how I experienced his nature, those years I was growing up in South Carolina. We kids had to bear the brunt of his stress leftover from THAT war.

One thing I'm so glad for is that I was able to teach both my parents and one brother to meditate on a trip home to see them in August 1977. Sometimes my dad would even sit and meditate with me on my visits home, out in a swing in the back yard, which faced down the hill to the pond on his land. That was certainly one of the best things I could do for my parents, to give them this technique to ease their stress.

When I learned to meditate, my mom recounted to me how her sister in Reno, my Aunt Marion, had made a statement to her, *"It's made a real human being out of her."* What? Wasn't I a human being before? I tried to be as polite, thoughtful, and helpful to her as I could, while I lived with them. I would clean the house when she told me to and anything else that she asked. Maybe she was just picking up a happier, lighter vibration in me once I was meditating.

I will always be so grateful and appreciative throughout my life to my aunt and uncle in Reno for taking me in when they did, having me live with them for four years and supporting me for my first two years in college. They made a huge positive difference in my life at a most critical junction point, growing up. I would not be who I am today without their practical help and intellectual influence. I sure do miss them, as they passed on many years ago.

When one door closes – sometimes we as human beings can feel that we've run out of ideas and don't know what our next step should be. I've learned that if we can cultivate our faith and really listen to the still small voice within, the guidance eventually bubbles up to the surface. I give thanks for that guidance. I literally don't know where I'd be without it. The more

I listen to it, the more aligned with Natural Law I feel, and the more smoothly life flows. This has brought me the insight to move at certain times to certain places, where I've met the friends I was supposed to meet there. When we can get our own fears out of the way, it really is a delightful process.

Negative thoughts and worry are coming from the lower self, anyway. I don't intend to let that lower self rule my life. Each time I have "stepped out in faith" as the saying goes, it seems that God, or the Universal Intelligence, has rewarded me greatly. That is the only way to find true and lasting peace of mind, to be in tune with, and in agreement with, that divine guidance. I am grateful every day for all who have brought spiritual light and wisdom into my life. It feels like I must be doing something right to have the blessings of good health, great friends, finally a home for myself in the beautiful town of Sedona, Arizona, with its exquisite natural beauty of the red rocks here, and such interesting spiritual people to get to know.

What is next is yet to unfold but I continue to trust in the Inner Guidance that comes to me. I realize now that it is just the small-self mind, the intellect and ego that wants to insist on "having all the answers" before making any decisions or taking any actions. That safety-and-security approach to life does not foster joy and the sense of freedom within which we all cherish. I have many techniques now for lifting myself up and over those types of thoughts and impulses when they arise. One does need to stay vigilant as a steward and thoughtful overseer of one's own spiritual growth. That is especially true in these times with so much upheaval in the environment from various levels of society, both domestic and international, which our consciousness is bombarded with each night, if we watch the daily news.

May everyone have such good guides and teachers as I have been blessed to have. My curiosity has also been a blessing to keep my mind open to learning new things and expanding my world by doing so. "The Road Less Traveled" certainly could be a fitting theme for my journey in this lifetime.

There have been a few uncomfortable detours (such as Robb's six years in prison) but overall it has been an interesting and worthwhile adventure, and definitely not boring. I go back to my motto, *"The Best is Yet to Come."*

Chapter Twenty
Guidance Came to Write This Book

A new teacher I met here shared a funny saying, *"One thing about Sedona, no one will ever consider you weird here."* Well, that is certainly a relief to hear. They didn't consider me too weird in Boulder, Colorado either, during my eighteen years there. I recently read a quote, *"When I told you I was normal, I may have slightly exaggerated."* Ah, it feels so good to laugh. Whatever type of drama or intensity has happened in my life, I've always been able to bounce back and get into that place of laughter again. It is such a rich dimension to enjoy – laughing at ourselves is often the best medicine.

Writing this book has been very liberating for me, as I had hoped it would be. I would love for my story to go worldwide but whatever happens with this book, I've had the pleasure of visiting special memories, which feels like visiting old friends in a way. I am delighted when I see leaps of growth for anyone I know, as well as for myself when I grow. It is amazing how writing one's memoirs - perhaps, the first one in a series - can feel so healing. It's an experience I would encourage anyone who has the slightest desire to write to embark upon.

I have always felt that more communication is better than less, and contributes to resolving misunderstandings and confusion in most situations. Of course, there are always those who want to take their marbles and play elsewhere and they are welcomed to do that. My Uncle Jennings used to observe me nearly like a science experiment when I lived with them in Reno. He told me once that I was a catalyst. Oh Lord, what is that?

Apparently it is someone who causes changes to happen by just showing up in a given scenario or situation.

One thing I've noticed about myself is that I am a type of risk taker – not physical risks – no, far from it. I have gambled on love and in doing so, I do feel it has improved the lives of those I loved, even the ones who couldn't really accept that energy from me. No matter, at some level their soul "gets it," I feel sure. *"It is certainly better to have loved and lost than to have never loved at all."* That is true to me now. What I've seen of the ones who bottle up their hearts and don't let any real love flow in or out, they are very miserable people. For Love is the universal energy and reason for living on this planet. It makes the world go 'round and lights up the hearts, smiles, and eyes of those who give and receive it. Here's to Love.

Sometimes learning to love ourselves is the hardest job of all. We can more easily forgive others of their trespasses than we can forgive ourselves of the slightest imperfections. In our culture, most of us have grown up with the implied societal "rules" that it is not okay to make a mistake. Imperfection is very much frowned upon. However, that is the only way most of us actually learn – through trial and error. We find out what works and doesn't work for us, more often than not, the hard way.

In Robb's case, he had decided to "color outside of the lines" and he surely paid the price for it, more than he had counted on, I'm sure. He had made one colossal mistake, which carried a big, heavy-duty penalty per the laws of the land, but I still knew he was a good person, kind, decent, and lovable. Not too many people though, were willing to see him through my eyes at that time. No wonder certain friends just melted away out of my life. I've always been a very loyal person, through thick and thin, so losing friends was one more level of loss to contend with then, on top of the gigantic loss I was already feeling.

When we were young, Robb was athletic and full of energy. My passion came out in other arenas, such as politics and a concern about much-needed social changes. I'd love to put an end to all wars, for one thing. One time, while the Vietnam War was going on, we university students organized a peace march down the main street in town, right under the "Reno – Biggest Little City in the World" arch. This was a silent march. We wore black armbands and each of us carried a lit candle. I felt it was such a profound and dignified statement about how we felt about the war. I would have only participated in a silent march, in fact. The only thing not silent was the shouts and curses at us from the drunken tourists on the sidewalks. Didn't they have sons or daughters who were over there in the war, being killed or maimed? Didn't they know someone in their circle of friends and family who did?

Their unconscious reactions did not deter us or cause any disruptions. We proceeded to the end of the march, as peacefully as we had started. It was clear that not everyone was with us, but it felt good to make that peaceful, silent statement that we did. I wondered how anyone could be FOR war. President Eisenhower was the first one to coin the phrase "military-industrial complex" and warn us about the societal evils of that structure taking us over, which it seems to me that it has, and I feel our country is much worse off for that. Ike certainly had some amazing insights to see that far into the future and predict what he did.

After the skyjacking, I didn't have the energy to get involved or put any more time into big picture social changes. What had changed were all our plans to live a happy life together. I didn't care at that point what jobs we got and I had no career ambitions anymore, after giving up the dream of a doctorate degree in anthropology. I just wanted to be happy, and enjoy being in love. My only outlet before I learned to meditate was journaling.

Wouldn't it be nice if we were all born perfect? Yet then, what would be the purpose of being "born" out of a heavenly realm? We could have just stayed there. David used to say he couldn't see WHY, with all the horrible things that take place on this Earth, all of "man's inhumanity to man," wars, and the like, why did the Creator create Creation in the first place? Why not just stay in that divine, unmanifest, energetic void of perfect Beingness? Well, in a way, those were very intelligent questions, but also there he goes again...David, questioning the wisdom of God. Our meditation program founder had told us that Creation was for the play and display of God, bringing that divine spark within each of us into human form and seeing what our free wills would make of it.

Well, one jolly big mess, from the looks of things, is the answer. Sometimes as the years go by, I can understand David's question more. We humans could really make this a Heaven on Earth if we would learn to love one another and act from there.

David was not my first boyfriend, but he was certainly my First Love, and most of us always have a warm spot in our hearts for our first loves. He was not interested in having a feet-on-the-ground, real-life relationship, so I had to stop waiting around for the impossible and go for a love that was real.

I give credit to Robb's good behavior while in prison, plus my teaching him TM and him faithfully practicing it for the first six months as I had urged, for his release on parole just six months after learning TM. Perhaps I should also give myself a little credit for the type of love and support I'd sent his way for so many years. He had written one touching letter, realizing that I may have to move on with my life and not be able to wait for him forever. He asked me to still help him, if that were to happen. I shared that letter earlier. I did my best to live up to his earnest request for help, when he most needed it.

He was more practical than I was in some ways. I was the more idealistic one. We were a good balance and help for each other, in that way. Perhaps idealistically, I wanted him to be perfect, or different, or more like me than he was when he got out of prison. I am sorry if I put too much pressure on him to fit into my pristine meditation-teacher world. That is the path I had chosen to take, and needed to take, to keep my head together while he was locked away for such a long time.

We had become the people we were then, by age 28, and that was that. Maybe we got married out of some sense of loyalty, or perhaps because of remembering who we both used to be, when we were younger, before all the trouble happened.

Chapter Twenty-One
The Big Picture

E thlyn Luce had told me in that reading many years before, that my Life Purpose was to gain Enlightenment, and she said that while this is ultimately everyone's purpose, that in this life I was going like a comet toward this lofty spiritual goal. Maybe that's true from the soul level, but tell that to my human self! All I've ever really wanted was to be happily married and share a deep heart and soul connection with my mate. Is that too much to ask for, dear God?

"First deserve and then desire" was a saying I heard around TM circles, so I strove to be deserving. Another saying we heard was *"Yogastah Kuru Karmani"* which means, "Established in Being, perform action." Okay, I strove for that, too.

Sometimes it would be nice to take a "vacation" from all this growth stuff, you know. Which reminds me of something funny that we were told on our six-months TM teacher-training course – we were in class every single day, all day long, when not meditating in our rooms. We felt a need for a day off once a week, to do our laundry, write letters home and just rest, so we made a request for that. The word we got back was that the TM Founder's reply was, *"A day off from what?"* Oh, ha, ha, ha – how many times I have thought of that when asking the Universe the type of questions I just posed above. None of us get a day off from the need for growth or lessons here on Earth School, from my experience. However, that doesn't stop me from whining that I would really LIKE one.

Another funny thing that will stay in my memory and comes to mind on occasion is something David said. He was referring to his having to go and fight in Vietnam when he was so against war. He *said, "I don't know what I did in a past life to deserve this, but I sure am sorry!"* In future conversations we would both have occasion to refer to that saying as we each faced various life challenges.

Few veterans of any war talk much about their experiences "over there." These bottled-up memories and experiences will eventually poison their bodies, partnerships or family life, if not healed and released. We have this awful cycle of fathers not being there, not being "present" in one way or another, for their sons or daughters, and then the male children, especially, are wounded by this lack of quality role model for what it's like to be a husband and a dad. Thus, the boys repeat those patterns of emotional distance in the families they create when they grow up, get married, and have children.

I'm saying that between the scars of war inflicted on the men of our own generation and then the often-times Distant Defense pattern wounds they experienced from their relationships with their fathers which mold how they turn out, what chance do we women have?

It takes a lot of inner work to become self-aware, to be an emotionally, psychologically, and spiritually aware person. Because it is typically a painful and messy ordeal to get from Square One to where we want to be, in order to be the people we came here to be, most people avoid it like the plague.

My generation, the Flower Children, and hippies of the '60s and early '70s, we really did have a vision of the world as a more peaceful place. *"Love all the people, man"* – the music of our time reflected our spirit and intentions to make this a better world. I was certainly not the only one out there with that focus.

"I want to fly like an eagle, to the sea. Fly like an eagle, let my spirit carry me, fly like an eagle and be free. ....Time keeps on slipping, slipping, slipping into the future...." Ah, I love that great song from the Steve Miller Band. I could really relate to this message.

Some of the main spiritual lessons that I have learned so far on my life journey:

1. Spiritual initiations can take many forms, including what's often called the Dark Night of the Soul. We can get through if we keep our faith strong.

2. The smartest question to ask is, *"Dear God, what am I supposed to learn in this situation?"* (It's too easy to see what we think the OTHERS are supposed to learn, but it is not our place to teach them, nor to set ourselves up as judge, jury and executioner.)

3. Forgiveness is always necessary. That includes forgiveness of one's self, which most of us usually find tougher than forgiving others.

4. Love alone is not enough, when it comes to romantic relationships. If you are around my age, you have probably learned this the hard way by now.

5. Everything really does happen for a reason.

I believe that when we do not get what we want or pray for, that is a sign that we have some more work to do on ourselves in order to be ready to receive that gift, and to appreciate it once we receive it. Either that, or the Creator has a bigger and better plan in mind for us.

One thing I had to learn was not to feel lonely. The more I cultivated those deep inner experiences, the more at peace I became.

We can only keep doing the "next-best-right thing to do" as our Inner Guidance delivers that to us. Just recently, my guidance has been to share my story in this book with all of you, so that is what I have done.

At the time, my next-best step after Robb left Austin, the marriage, and me, was to get myself moved to the more dynamic, stimulating meditation community in Silver Spring,

Maryland, a suburb of Washington, D. C. After a year and a half in Texas, I was on my way. I didn't have a job but I lined up a room to rent in a meditator's home.

The move there went smoothly. Once again, there I was traveling solo, driving across the country to yet another "new beginning." I was now age 36.

It was July 29, 1986, that I left Austin for the drive east, and I arrived in Silver Spring on August 1, 1986, to begin my new life there. Along the way, these thoughts and feelings about Robb came to me in a short poem:

> *"Something's out of tune;*
> *You're on the Dark Side of the Moon,*
> *Above the sailing airships,*
> *Communications are eclipsed.*
> *Free form floating in limitless space,*
> *Memory holds you, a soul, and a face."*

But that part of life was over. I was off, heading out on another grand adventure, to a bright, exciting new set of experiences in our nation's capitol. I still felt the best was yet to come.

At that time when I was moving from Austin, Texas, to Silver Spring, Maryland, though, I still had much to learn. I was hoping that my fresh start in the Washington, D. C. area would bring the excitement, connections, and answers to life's riddles that I sought. There were certainly some wonderful new friendships awaiting me there, and many knowledge courses to expand my spiritual growth and sense of community. I was able to make the contributions that were important to me by attending numerous international World Peace Assemblies including some with over 5000 people from all over the world. There were some wonderful times for me in the six years I was to spend there.

One of the most exciting first steps to my new life was applying for a job as the Assistant to the Ad Sales Director of *Newsweek* Magazine. Amazingly, I got that job and was soon working at 1750 Pennsylvania Avenue, just half a block from the White House. My boss, Joe Werner, was a wonderful man, to top off this good fortune. This was a sure sign to me that I had moved to the right place.

For those of you reading this who are from my generation, I'll say that like you, I am the product of my times, a child of our generation, who wanted the same things as you did - a beautiful and loving world in which to live, for us all. My story is just a little bit different than most, since I became The Skyjacker's Wife.

I could still dream. I could still believe in love and have hopes for a brighter future. There was a new chapter of possibilities for me to explore, as I headed down the highway alone. Then I thought about David, and wondered what he was up to after all these years. My curiosity was getting the better of me, and I knew that I had to find out.

Epilogue

In recent years, I've read some interesting and moving accounts of near-death experiences. Some of these stories offer intricate details of the writer's "journey" to the Other Side, and back to waking consciousness.

One story that I find most touching and compelling is that of Matthew Ward, as told to his mother, the author Suzanne Ward. Her first book is *Matthew, Tell Me about Heaven: A Firsthand Description of the Afterlife.*

She explains how her son Matthew died in an accident when he was age 17, and how her grief led her to consult with readers who could "talk with" Matthew from his new home in the Higher Dimensions. After some years of relying on others, she realized she could experience telepathic messages directly from Matthew.

One of the hardest conversations, which he knew was coming, finally occurred when he had to let her know that the two of them, before either was born, had as souls "agreed to" this drama playing out just the way it did, with his tragic early death in this lifetime. This mother's heart was broken and she was trying to understand why her precious son had to be taken from her so young in his human life.

Her reaction to what he was now sharing with her was understandable: denial, anger, refusal to accept at first that they could have possibly made such an agreement. Gradually she came to understand that this was the case. The higher soul purpose to which they had been called became of universal service to humanity, as we get to read intricate details of life in this Heaven world in which Matthew now resides. His messages and the resultant books that have been channeled to his mother

Suzanne have inspired and brought comfort to so many readers.

In the course of writing my own story, I also had an awakening experience of, *"Oh no, Robb and I must have agreed to this set of challenging circumstances so that I could some day write a book about it, too!"* There is shock and denial when we discover that we are the participants in such a soul arrangement that has at its core the higher purpose of bringing spiritual awareness and emotional comfort to others who have suffered in similar ways.

"No, no, no! I would not have agreed to all that pain, loss and suffering!" is the first reaction from our human selves. Say it isn't so. I felt rebellious indignation to think I would have *"volunteered for such a mission."* If so, *"What was I thinking?"* on the Other Side that made me be foolhardy enough to take on this challenge? Not to mention Robb, taking on his role in this drama. My small self does not like it one little bit. I protest, I demand a recount, I appeal to the ladies and gentlemen of the celestial jury. PLEASE don't make me have to go through all this grief, agony, and emotional deprivation at such a young age when my life was supposed to be coming together in happy ways. It does not feel fair, I tell you. I was a good person and didn't deserve to have to go through that hell. It truly doesn't feel right to have to make such sacrifices. Did I really have to sacrifice my youth to write a damn book? God help me.

Okay, sometimes epiphanies are not the most graceful or fun things to go through. We are a combination of divine spirit and human beings. Sometimes the human part forgets that we are souls on a journey, and we do have a mission plan, and yes....like it or not, we accepted the script before we were born here. As distasteful as it seems, when our Far Memory gets shut down once we are born and the "fun begins," it appears from all the spiritual knowledge that I have gained, that we are willing actors, taking on our roles in the play of life.

Dr. Michael Newton's books, *Journey of Souls* and *Destiny of Souls,* give a fascinating account of what happens "between lifetimes." As a hypnotherapist with a regular practice, it was by accident that he found some patients giving reports of what they experienced in this in-between zone after one life journey had ended and as they were preparing for the current life.

It seems clear to me that we do have angels, guardian angels, Spirit Guides, teachers and a whole hierarchy of Light Beings who love us and nurture us with their compassionate wisdom as we prepare for our next "mission" on this Earth. *"Nothing is given to us greater than our ability to handle"* was one of my beloved spiritual teachers, Charlie Lute's, messages to us. I really do believe that is true, and the accounts in Dr. Newton's books chronicling our preparation time between lives supports this concept.

It is no fun to feel pain of any kind. We can learn the easy way or the hard way, based on how stubborn we choose to be while in Earth School. Apparently some of us have to be hit over the head pretty hard to wake up and "remember" who we are: Beings of Light and Love, and Children of God, here to grow, love, and help one another.

This book has required that I be quite vulnerable to open up and share this very personal story, that's for sure. I sincerely hope that relating my own painful ordeal, which led to much spiritual growth and lessons learned, will bring helpful encouragement and understanding to many. If I could get through all of my challenges, so can you. What a long way I had to go and to grow, once my youthful dreams were falling through the skies, over Reno.

Author's Notes

T he evening Sun illuminates the magnificent red rocks of Sedona as I write this. The mystical vortex energy of these gorgeous natural formations has drawn spiritual pilgrims here for decades. I feel blessed to live just down the road from some of them.

It is so clear to me now that I felt guided to move here for the specific purpose of sharing my story in book form at long last. Sedona, Arizona has proven the perfect inspirational environment for this book to come forth. It has been waiting to be born for a long time.

I did not know of Tom Bird and his Author Retreat program until a few months after I arrived here. When I attended one of his introductory talks, I got to experience for myself the Author Within state of consciousness he described. At that time I had a real "aha" moment. During those initial exercises that evening, this book started pouring out of me onto the pages of my notebook at a very fast pace. I subsequently enrolled in Tom's three and a half day Write Your Best Seller in a Weekend retreat and had the most profound experience of witnessing, as it were, this book complete itself during that course.

The editing and revision process continued at home, using the techniques we were taught to stay in the Author Within state to allow the refinements to come from that same intuitive level of awareness.

Feelings of deep gratitude wash over me, as I contemplate how Divine Guidance so clearly led me to this point, and to this opportunity to share with you the details of my amazing journey.

Bibliography

1. *Lady Chatterley's Lover*, D. H. Lawrence, first published 1928.
2. *Shakespeare's Sonnets*, William Shakespeare, first published in 1609.
3. *The Skies Belong to Us; Love and Terror in the Golden Age of Hijacking*, Brenden L. Koerner, published June 18, 2013, Amazon.com.
4. Interview by Emerson Marcus, November 22, 2011, with Steve Dundas, former United Airline Agent at Reno-Tahoe International Airport.
5. *The Glass House*, Truman Capote and Wyatt Cooper, 1972.
6. *Life Magazine* final issue December 29, 1972, photos of all the skyjackers that year.
7. *Here and Hereafter*, Ruth Montgomery, Coward, McCann & Geoghegan, 1968.
8. *Many Mansions*, Gina Cerminara, 1950, republished 1988 by Signet.
9. *Love and God*, Maharishi Mahesh Yogi, MIU Press, 1973.
10. *Living, Learning & Loving*, Leo Buscaglia, Ph.D., Fawcett Columbine, 1982.
11. *Men Are From Mars/Women Are From Venus*, Dr. John Gray, Harper Collins Publishers, 1992.
12. *The Hunt for DB Cooper – An Interview with a So-Called Cooper Copycat – Skyjacker Robb Dolin Heady*, Bruce A. Smith, The Mountain News – WA, March 28, 2013.
13. *Matthew, Tell Me About Heaven: a First Hand Description of the Afterlife*, Suzanne Ward, Matthew Books, September 1, 2002.
14. Journey of Souls, Michael Newton, Ph. D., Llewellyn Publications, July, 1994.
15. *Destiny of Souls*, Michael Newton, Ph. D., Llewellyn Worldwide, May, 2000.

About the Author

M ary Stevenson has had a strong spiritual focus in her life since the age of 23 when she was taught to meditate at the Reno TM Center. She became a TM teacher on April 13, 1976, after six months of training in Europe. From the early 1970's, Mary organized or helped run meditation centers around the country, including in Reno, Nevada; Austin, Texas; Silver Spring, Maryland; and Boulder, Colorado. She also spent four years in the spiritual community of Fairfield, Iowa. For many years she regularly attended large world peace assemblies around the country to enjoy big group meditations with thousands of other TM practitioners from around the world.

She began studying Vedic Astrology in 1988, in order to understand why such life-changing major events occurred in her early life. These studies led to Mary giving much support, understanding and guidance to many thousands of people over the years, through her individual readings. She continues to provide Vedic Astrology sessions to clients near and far, which include the added value of her innate intuitive abilities.

She has special memories of her 18 years in Boulder, Colorado, hiking in the beautiful Rocky Mountains with so many dear friends there. Mary currently resides in Sedona, Arizona, where she enjoys attending yoga classes and being in Nature, hiking in the unique natural beauty of the Red Rock formations. In this, her first book, Mary shares the experiences of the special fourteen year period of her early life, for its potential to inspire others who may be going through a challenging or confusing time.

www.vedicstarcharts.com

www.watchyourstars.com

www.healingconnections.net

www.marystevensonauthor.com

Made in United States
Orlando, FL
11 February 2022

14711457R00091